The Charismatic Prayer Group:
A Handbook

The Charismatic Prayer Group: A Handbook

For Leaders, Members and Clergy

by

JOHN GUNSTONE

HODDER AND STOUGHTON
LONDON SYDNEY AUCKLAND TORONTO

Acknowledgments

I am grateful to the Editor of the *Church of Ireland
Gazette* for allowing me to use material from articles
previously published in that paper, and to
Charles Mortimer Giulbert, as Custodian of the
Standard Book of Common Prayer (Protestant
Episcopal Church of the U.S.A.) for permission to
quote from *Services for Trial: Authorised Alternatives to
Prayer Book Services* © (1971).

Contents

page

INTRODUCTION   9

Chapter

1 Forming the Group   13

2 Leading the Group   27

3 Receiving God's Word   42

4 Praying Together   57

5 Ministering to one Another   75

6 Testing the Spirits   88

7 Sharing in Ministry   102

8 Breaking Bread Together   118

9 Overseeing the Groups   132

10 Following the Spirit   147

CONCLUSION   157

Introduction

THE PRAYER GROUP is the outstanding feature of the current charismatic movement. Baptism with the Holy Spirit — renewal in the Spirit — is usually followed by a desire for closer unity in Christ with our fellow believers. The result is that, under the impulse of the Spirit, we gather with three, four, six or eight other Christians and read the Bible meditatively together, pray to hear God's word, and seek to serve him in one another and in society around us.

Not that the worship and activities of the local church mean any less to those who join charismatic prayer groups. On the contrary, renewal in the Spirit leads to a more joyful participation in the liturgy and a more lively membership of the congregation.

But the structures of most local churches do not give us the freedom to do some of the things that God seems to be calling us to do in these days of his Spirit's outpouring. For these things — they are described in this book — it is necessary to assemble in smaller groups. And so, in all parts of the world, charismatic prayer groups are forming and through them tens of thousands are entering into a fresh experience of the love and power of God in Jesus Christ.

We are shown in Acts how the gift of the Spirit at Pentecost, the preaching of Peter's first sermon, and the baptism of the converts resulted in the calling together of a Spirit-filled community within the old Israel and how that community proclaimed the Gospel of Jesus Christ in the ancient world. From this we learn that we are not renewed in order to have exciting experiences of the Spirit; we are renewed in order that the Church may participate more faithfully in the ministry and mission of Christ in society.

Strictly speaking, the gift of the Spirit to the individual Christian is not that individual's affair. The Spirit is given him for others. The movement of divine love within us is two-way: towards the Father through Jesus Christ, and towards those who are members of Christ's body (and, beyond that body, to all whom God has made).

Paul called this "participation in the Spirit". The Greek word that he used, *koinonia*, is a famous one in scriptural vocabulary. The Jerusalem Bible's translation evokes a sense of the unifying love of God implanting in believers an impulse to come together as one — "the Spirit we have in common".

That is why an experience of renewal is followed by a search for fellowship in the Spirit — and the charismatic prayer group is one of the maifestations of that search.

At their best, charismatic prayer groups are authentic forms of Christian community — a blessing to those who belong to them and to those around them. At their worst, they are cliquey and divisive, a thorn in the side of the local church.

Most are probably in between these extremes, slowly growing in maturity and moving hesitantly into demanding kinds of ministry in the name of Jesus Christ. As they respond to the guidance of God, they encounter difficulties — within their membership and in their relationships with those outside the group, particularly their parent congregations. But difficulties are not necessarily signs of failure or weakness; they can be the devil's attempts to thwart the work of God.

From my experience of groups in a parish where I was vicar, and from what I have learned as a member of a Christian community much involved with members of groups, I have seen the Lord remove difficulties or overcome them. This book describes a few of the ways in which he does this.

Obviously no two groups are alike and the situation of each is different. But some general lessons can be learned.

I have tried to illustrate from my experiences and from conversations I have had with members of prayer groups vital aspects of a group's formation and life — its initial coming together, its leadership, its acceptance of new members, its reflection on the word of God, and its response in prayer, in worship and in minstry to its own members and to those around it.

Let me emphasise, however, that the contents of this book are *only suggestions*. They do not provide a blueprint for any single prayer group. It is for the reader to discern what he can use and what he can disregard as he applies what I have written to his own circumstances.

I have included a special chapter for those parish priests and ministers who find charismatic prayer groups arising within their congregations or who initiate them as part of their pastoral work.

Finally, I have to say that I am not entirely happy with the title I have chosen for this book. It implies that there are some prayer groups which are charismatic and some which are not — and that I can't believe! Any group which comes together under the impulse of the Spirit is, in the proper sense of the word, charismatic. Indeed, since eternal life in Christ is a *charisma* ("the free gift of God is eternal life in Christ Jesus our Lord," Romans 6 : 23), every Christian is a charismatic and every congregation a charismatic group.

But we live in a commercial era of not-too-accurate, eye-catching labels, and for most Christians today the title indicates those for whom this book has been written. So it will have to stand. Thus, unfortunately, does economics dominate theology!

CHAPTER 1

Forming the Group

A YOUNG COUPLE I know in a Midlands town were baptised with the Holy Spirit. For some months they travelled many miles each week to attend a charismatic prayer group in a vicarage in a nearby city. Eventually they decided to form a group of their own, fixed an evening for it, and invited friends to attend.

The results were disappointing. A few came occasionally, but the group never cohered. Privately they discussed the names of people they might invite and begged to the Lord to send them: "Urge Jean to come, Father, she really needs it ... Move in the heart of Robert, Holy Spirit, he has so much to give ..."

But Jean and Robert and the others never came — or, if they did, attended only one or two meetings and then dropped out of the group.

One day, when the couple were reverently questioning the Lord why the group had not been established, he reminded them that, if the prayer group was to be their own project, done in their own way, it would fail; but if it was done in his way, it would grow and be fruitful.

They realised their error. All along they had regarded it as *their* group, dependent upon *their* efforts. But in reality it was the Lord's group. He had a plan for it. They should pray to be in that plan.

From that time things began to change. The couple stopped trying to "pray in" certain individuals. They simply asked God to send to the meetings those who were ready and who had hungry hearts. At the next group meeting a priest friend "happened" to call in; he joined in his first charismatic prayer fellowship and said later that a deep need had been met by the Holy Spirit through the petitions offered for him. Another person, hardly known to the couple, arrived the following week and became a regular member. The group slowly grew and matured.

The Initial Group

A charismatic prayer group may begin after a number of people have attended a rally or a conference on the renewal movement or when they read books on baptism with the Holy Spirit. When the initiative to meet is taken spontaneously by a few in this way, we may believe that God is calling them to discover more of his love in a closer fellowship with each other.

But more often it is an individual or a married couple who, after experiencing a pentecostal-type renewal, look round the congregation of which they are a part and wonder how a group is to be formed. Should they invite one or two friends to their home one evening? Should they ask the vicar to put a notice in the parish newsletter?

Any of these ways may be right — and, as we shall see, there is a special reason for keeping the parish priest or minister informed of what is happening — but first we must learn to let the initiative for forming a group come from God, as my acquaintances in the Midlands realised. If we have entered into a fuller awareness of the Lord's presence and power in our lives, this can be an opportunity for putting that experience to the test.

"Where two or three are gathered in my name, there am I in the midst of them" (Mathew 18: 20). This saying of Jesus is quoted so frequently with reference to any sort of Christian meeting that the implication of the words "in my name" can be lost to us. In the Bible to do anything "in the name" of God is to do it under his authority and direction. To gather in Christ's name, therefore, is to come together according to his purposes.

God does not necessarily call into a group those who happen to be friends or who happen to see a notice in a newsletter. Indeed, he seems to delight in creating a unique fellowship out of differing personalities — people who are not normally attracted to one another. Who could have imagined in the political situation of Judaea in the first century A.D. that Christ would summon round him a band of twelve men including individuals so radically opposed to

one another as Simon the Zealot and Matthew the
tax-gatherer?

People with differing personalities and outlooks
can become a richly-equipped group within the
Church when they are brought together and gifted by
the Holy Spirit. On visits to Ireland I have discovered
this in charismatic groups which embraced Roman
Catholics and Protestants in Belfast. The love I experienced among their members was intensely
moving and impossible to describe.

There is no technique in forming a prayer group.
What matters is our faithful expectation of what God
can do. The personal invitation or the notice in the
newsletter may be the right way to initiate a group,
but that way must have been prayed about first. We
should ask the Spirit to guide into the group the
people of his choice, not ours, and to give us the love
and discernment to accept them in Christ's name.

Generally speaking, if the method we adopt to
form the group causes us anxiety, so that we have to
rush around reminding individuals of meetings, we
can assume we are out of step with the Spirit's working. God's purposes are not fulfilled through hurry
and worry. The right method will be that which gives
us an inner peace and confidence in him. Then, when
the group begins to form, its members will come into
an atmosphere which will help them to relax as they
wait upon the Lord.

It is only too easy for a group to come together in
anything but a prayerful way. Some people come to a
prayer group out of mere curiosity. They want to
know more about the apparently unusual goings-on

they have heard rumoured, and their interest is on the same level as a mild curiosity about psychism and the occult. While a few of these may be converted from curiosity to commitment, the rest will remain like the Athenians to whom Paul preached — on the lookout for novelty and unwilling to accept the discipline of Jesus Christ.

Then there are some who come to a prayer group primarily out of an awareness of their own inadequacy. They hope that they will somehow be made better by a spiritual experience. While it is true that the Holy Spirit will remove obstacles to psychological maturity and heal personality disorders, there is nothing automatic about this. Skilled and specific psychiatric help may be needed. Then, as the intellectual, emotional and intuitive aspects of the personality become more integrated, there may be a real growth in the individual, a new readiness to be of service to God, and a more spiritual basis for participation in prayer.

And there are some who join a prayer group because of a feeling of emotional dissatisfaction and a desire for spiritual experience as an end in itself. In an age which shouts that one must have significant feelings about life, many people — especially the young — look for stimulation from outside sources — drugs, sex, noise, or mystical experience. They may come to a prayer group looking for "spiritual kicks". Such a motive can be transformed with patience into a real quest for God involving repentance and faith — but again much discipline is required on the way.

Our motives for seeking fellowship are doubtless mixed and often unconscious. Can we be sure that we, or anyone else, are joining a prayer group purely out of a desire to grow together in the Spirit? If I pressed this question too much I could be accused of seeking to exclude from a group those in real need of Christian ministry. This is certainly not my intention, as I hope the rest of this book will demonstrate. All I am saying is that, at the beginning of its life, a group cannot carry the burden of too many dependent or casual members — those who are unable to contribute to its activities either because their own personal needs are too great or because their interest is only peripheral.

In time a group of six or eight Christians who are learning to pray together and to trust one another will be able to take into its fellowship those whose needs are greater than their contributions. But the initial group must establish itself first. (And, even then, it will not be able to cope with more than one or two highly dependent members at a time, otherwise its time and energy will be swamped with their demands.)

The Meeting

Students may find it convenient to use a room in college for a prayer meeting, and in less affluent churches a group may gather in a small hall or vestry, but most charismatic prayer groups seem to meet in one another's homes.

There is everything to be said for this. Reasonable

comfort and domestic surroundings help people to relax. Folding garden chairs can be used to supplement the sitting-room suite and stored away when not required.

A group which goes from house to house should have an understanding among its members about the kind of refreshment provided. One hostess, in a burst of enthusiasm, might prepare a lavish spread at one of the first meetings, and then the next hostess may feel that she should do the same. Coffee or tea and biscuits are all that are needed, unless something substantial has to be got ready in special circumstances.

Over a period regular meetings in the same house add to the occupier's bills for heating and lighting, and arrangements should be made to compensate him. If a collection is taken occasionally, the surplus cash can be used for the hire of tapes and cassettes and to build up a small library.

Advice about the frequency of meetings is not easy to give. People's circumstances vary so much. A group which is not prepared to meet at least once a fortnight is not likely to grow together very quickly. In time it may want to meet weekly, if not more often. A programme of weekly meetings with seasonal breaks is better than one of fortnightly meetings continued through the year.

Once the initial group fixes a day in the week for its meeting, it is wise to stick to it. If a certain evening is inconvenient for someone who is interested in joining we may believe that, if God wants him to come, his personal arrangements will be changed, or he will be linked to another group. In areas where there are many retired people, groups can meet in the morning or in the afternoon. Elsewhere groups should meet when husbands and wives can come together.

When our group has assembled, we must guard against wasting time. Casual conversation has its place in any fellowship, but we should ensure that it does not divert us from the main purpose of the meeting. We can arrange social gatherings for the group on other occasions — a meal in a restaurant or a visit to the theatre. During regular meetings we should try to begin at a certain time, even if one or two persist in arriving late.

Similarly, we should have a fixed hour for officially ending the meeting. We could agree to terminate the proceedings at ten o'clock but allow those who wish to stay for further prayer. A possible time-table might be:

7.45 p.m.	Assembly
8.00	Bible reading followed by reflection.
8.45	Prayer.
9.45	Coffee.
10.00	Further prayer for those who wish stay.

But as the group becomes more open to the Spirit's leading and to the needs of its members, the time-table may change from meeting to meeting. What is vital, however, is that we have time to reflect on God's word, to listen to what he is saying to us, and to respond in confession, petition and praise, as the

Spirit guides us. This planned opportunity for corporate spiritual communion with God is the mainspring of all our other activities as Christians, both as members of the Church and as individuals.

New Members

Once the initial group is formed, there is often a period when the membership remains fairly static. It is as if the Lord is giving us a chance to grow together in his Spirit before he demands more of us. Then others begin to enquire if they can join the group and inevitably the question arises, Do we accept everyone who wants to come?

Again, we have to adopt the same attitude towards this problem that we adopted towards the formation of the group. Since the Lord called the original members into its fellowship, we believe he will lead others into it. Then our group will increase with a growth that is from God. Anything like a recruitment drive to keep numbers up is unwise.

Groups devise their own ways of introducing new people. Some accept anyone whom a member brings along. Others ask that names be discussed before an invitation is made. And others have a system whereby members bring guests so that the newcomer can meet the group before he or she is invited to become a regular member. What matters in each case is that the group should seek God's guidance according to the situation in which it finds itself.

A process of prayerful selection of new members is strange to many Christian gatherings. We are not happy about anything that hints at exclusivism. We like to put *All Welcome* signs over everything we do.

A further complication is that charismatics are sometimes accused of dividing the local congregation into "first-class" and "second-class" Christians — the "first-class" being those who go to prayer groups and the "second-class" those who don't!

These are serious difficulties. But we have to remember that open-ended gatherings are rarely effective for the more costly demands of Christian discipleship. The telephone Samaritans, for example, are very careful in their choice of volunteers. When we invite someone to a charismatic prayer group, we are not inviting them to a cosy evening in someone's home. We are inviting them to a meeting in which we may together learn to be more open to the Spirit, and the consequences of this are usually a good deal more testing than what is experienced in open church meetings.

Misunderstanding will almost certainly arise between the group and the congregation — but these are opportunities for Christian love to conquer the divisive tactics of the devil. We shall discuss this in a later chapter.

When the wrong person does find his way into a prayer group, his presence can be destructive.

A group in Manchester was visited one evening by a comparative stranger who, from the first, attempted to dominate the proceedings. He claimed he had been sent by God to teach the members more about the Holy Spirit. During the Bible reading he monopolised the discussion, expounding strange teachings, and during the prayers he joined in frequently, speaking in tongues and giving his own interpretations — which substantiated what he had been telling the group!

At the next meeting the leaders attempted to check him, but without success. He was obviously unwilling to submit to any discipline.

After that, the group began to wilt. The onslaught of the newcomer's personality was too much for them. So before the next meeting the leaders, two men and their wives (the group was large — twenty plus) met to pray about the problem. They asked the Lord either to show them how they could help the newcomer or to deliver them from him.

The evening of the third meeting arrived. The members came to the house as usual, but with a notable lack of enthusiasm. Conversation was half-hearted as they sipped their coffee. Every ear was cocked for the now familiar *rat-at-at* on the front door.

Eight o'clock came and went. The minutes ticked by . . . Quarter past . . . Half past . . .

Suddenly the group realised that it was wasting time. They began their meeting in the normal way and soon the newcomer was forgotten . . .

He did not turn up that evening, and he never came again.

Family Involvement

Membership of a charismatic prayer group is more intrusive into our domestic life than ordinary churchgoing. The Christian wife of a non-practising or unbelieving husband, for example, finds herself torn between her duty to her family and her growing fellowship with the group. A similar problem arises when a Christian husband or wife is suspicious of the charismatic movement in which their spouse is involved.

Situations like these require loving patience and tact — the fruits of the Spirit. No Christian should ever put a group before his or her partner. The charism of marriage is itself a precious gift from God to be cherished and developed. If a group is not supporting one of its members to be a better husband or wife, then it is better that he or she should leave the group.

Fortunately, most people are tolerant of their partner's Christian practices and membership of a group need not create undue difficulties. The wife may have to accept the fact that she cannot be so involved in the group's life as she might be if her husband was a member of it. On the other hand, she will find the prayer and ministry of the group a welcome support in the midst of everyday problems. It may be possible to introduce the husband to the group by bringing him to meetings of a social nature occasionally.

Parents who belong to prayer groups tend to think of their children as hindrances rather than members when the evening for the meeting arrives. If the children are young, mother tries to get them to bed before the meeting starts; if they are older, father persuades them to sit in another room with the volume of the radio or the TV turned low.

But this is to deny them invaluable experiences at an impressionable age. Groups ought to work out ways of involving younger children in their meetings for a while before bed-time. Teenagers should be allowed to come to the meetings, if they wish. One seventeen-year-old, who declared he had no belief in God, was intrigued by the group that met in his home. He joked about it to his parents for the first week or so; then he asked if he might attend, and within a short time committed his life to Jesus Christ and received the Holy Spirit.

A Group Conference

The fellowship of a prayer group is powerfully strengthened if its members are able to go away together for a few days. It may be that they can arrange to go on holiday, with plans to spend time each day in Bible reading and prayer. Or, another time, they can organise a weekend conference at a centre to review their group life and to seek God's will for the future.

We welcome many such groups at Whatcombe House. A typical programme looks like this:

Friday

7.00 p.m.   Dinner.

8.30   Introductory Session. Prayer and praise, with notices and explanation of plan of weekend conference.

Saturday

8.30 a.m.	Breakfast.
10.00	Worship and Bible Study.
11.00	Coffee.
11.30	Session 2. Lecture on topic that concerns the group and its life.
1.00 p.m.	Lunch.
	Afternoon free.
4.30	Tea.
5.00	Session 3. Open discussion.
6.30	Dinner.
8.00	Evening meeting, talk, prayer and praise.

Sunday

8.30 a.m.	Breakfast.
10.00	Worship and Bible Study.
11.00	Coffee.
11.30	Session 4. Discussion and summing-up.
1.00 p.m.	Lunch.
2.30	Eucharist with final address.
4.00	Tea and depart.

Living together, even only for two days, gives the group a brief taste of community with one another which can have considerable influence on them as individuals. Often a group will look back on such a conference as an important experience in the development of their corporate life and ministry.

CHAPTER 2

Leading the Group

THE EFFECTIVENESS of a charismatic prayer group depends largely on the leadership it experiences. Of all the spiritual gifts bestowed by God on his people, the charism of leadership is one of the most vital for the building up and sustaining of the life of the Church.

We do not always think of leadership as a charism in the same way that we think of speaking in tongues or healing as spiritual gifts. We can be vividly aware of God's presence in a prayer group when a member is prophesying, but we are not so aware of his presence when the leader says, "Let's begin, shall we?" Yet without the gift of leadership exercised in this simple way — calling the group together to begin the meeting — many of the other charisms would be inoperative.

Leadership is mentioned in two of Paul's list of spiritual gifts. The first is in Romans 12: 8. Here the apostle was developing his teaching on Christians as members of the body of Christ and their dependence upon one another, urging them to exercise the particular charisms God had given them. Among the seven he listed by way of examples was *proistemi*. Unfortunately the *Revised Standard Version* translates this as, "He who gives aid with zeal." The *New English Bible* is clearer: "If you are a leader, exert yourself to lead."

The second reference is among the list of charisms in I Corinthians 12: 28, "administrators". The Greek world, *kybernesis*, is from a nautical background. It means "to steer" a ship, and from it we derive the modern term "cybernetics", the study of control systems which forms the scientific basis for the development of computers. The *New English Bible* translates the word as, "Power to guide (others)".

Like other spiritual gifts, the gift of leadership is for the benefit of others. It is not a personal honour. Any leader among Christians shares in the sacrificial leadership of Jesus Christ as the Messiah of God. "Whoever would be first among you must be slave of all. For the Son of Man also came not to be served but to serve, and to give his life as a ransom for many" (Mark 10: 44–45). The papal title of "servant of the servants of God" says exactly what leadership means in the Church.

This is as true of unofficial or "unordained" leadership as it is of the ordained leadership of the Church. The charism of leadership has been, and still is, exercised in different ways. From the beginning it has been discerned as a more or less permanent charism in some whom God has called, and these men (and women in a few denominations) have been ordained into an office which authorised them to act as a leader in the Church. But the basis of that office is the spiritual gift of leadership.

This is expressed in the *Agreed Statement on the Doctrine of the Ministry:*

> Just as the original apostles did not choose themselves but were chosen and commissioned by Jesus, so those who are ordained are called by Christ in the Church and through the Church. Not only is their vocation from Christ but their qualification for exercising such a ministry is the gift of the Spirit: "our sufficiency is from God, who has qualified us to be ministers of a new covenant, not in a written code but in the Spirit" (2 Corinthians 3: 5–6). This is expressed in ordination, when the bishop prays God to grant the gift of the Holy Spirit and lays hands on the candidate as the outward sign of the gifts bestowed*

The charism is akin to the function of a father in a family. According to 1 Timothy 3: 5 a man's ability as a natural father is a pointer as to his suitability as a spiritual leader. For a man who does not know how to manage (*proistemi* in the original epistle) his own household is not fit to be an elder in the Church. (In passing, it is worth noting that a married couple who are united in Christ often make very satisfactory joint

---

* *Ministry and Ordination — a Statement on the Doctrine of the Ministry agreed by the Anglican-Roman Catholic International Commission*, S.P.C.K., 1973, p. 9.

leaders of a prayer group, complementing one another in the pastoral care of the group as they do in the care of their family.)

Since leadership is a gift from God, it should be respected. "We beseech you to respect those who labour among you and are over you (*proistemenous* = 'the ones taking the lead') in the Lord and admonish you, and to esteem them very highly in love because of their work" (I Thessalonians 5: 12–13). While this does not mean that the members of the group should agree with everything the leader proposes, it does suggest that awkward, unwarranted opposition to the leader is dishonouring to God. Without leaders, we would not be able to fulfil the particular work to which God calls us in his Church.

The Choice of Leader

But how do we discern the charism of leadership, in ourselves or in others? (For the rest of this chapter I shall assume I am addressing those who are or who may be called to exercise the role of leader in a prayer group.)

The ordination services of the Church can help us in answering this question. Enshrining scriptural teaching about the gift of leadership as it has been revealed through the Church's age-long reflection on the word of God, these services provide three valuable guidelines on the discernment of leadership in a Christian community.

The first guideline is that you should be convinced that God is calling you to lead the group.

"I heard the voice of the Lord saying, 'Whom shall I send, and who will go for us?' Then I said, 'Here am I! Send me!' And he said, 'Go' " (Isaiah 6: 8–9). The prophet recognised the need and, after his purification by the seraphim, offered himself to fulfil that need. In other words, he was convinced that with God's help he could perform the ministry. This guideline is recognised in the Church of England's ordination service when the candidate is asked, "Do you think in your heart that you be truly called, according to the will of our Lord Jesus Christ, and the order of this Church of England, to the order and ministry of priesthood?"

If, seeing the need for a leader in a group, you feel an inclination to accept that responsibility yourself, then this may well be God's call to you. I must add, of course, that the desire to lead should be part of a greater desire to serve others: both unhealthy ambition and undue modesty are likely to deflect you from God's purpose if you allow either to dominate your ideas.

The second guideline is that the group should be willing to accept you as their leader.

"Pick out from among you seven men of good repute, full of the Spirit and of wisdom" (Acts 6: 3). This was the instruction to the apostolic Church when it required further leaders to serve its needs. The choice of the people was to be God's choice. The principle is not well demonstrated in the Church of England's ordination service,* but in the new ordinal

* Technically it is when the archdeacon presents the candidates to the bishop at the beginning of the service. He does this on behalf

drawn up for the Episcopal Church of the USA the bishop, before he lays hands on the candidate, asks the congregation, "Is he worthy?" The rubric in the service says: "The people respond with a loud voice saying these or other words, several times, 'He is worthy!' "

If you are the one who initiated the group, those who come will probably accept your leadership — the fact that they have responded to your invitation indicates this. If, however, it is a case of your assuming leadership in an already existing group, you should insist that the members of the group have an opportunity to discuss and pray about the matter (in your absence) before committing yourself. In any small group there will rarely be more than one or two possible candidates for the job of leadership, and one should emerge in the common mind of the group as the most suitable.

The third guideline is that you are acceptable as leader of the group within the wider Christian fellowship of which its members are a part.

"These they set before the apostles, and they prayed and laid their hands upon them" (Acts 6: 6). After the "deacons" had been chosen by the congregation in Jerusalem, they were accepted and authorised by the apostles. In doing this, the apostles expressed both the will of God and the approval of the whole Church. The bishop does a similar act in

---

of the people after the reading of the *Si Quis* in the parish in which the men are to serve their titles. (The *Si Quis*, like the banns of marriage, provides people with an opportunity for objecting to a man's ordination — not with an opportunity for selecting a leader.)

the ordination service: "Receive the Holy Ghost for the office and work of a priest in the Church of God, now committed unto thee by the imposition of our hands."

Applied to the leadership of a prayer group, it means that if you are invited to assume the responsibility of leader, you should at least discuss it with your parish priest or minister and perhaps also with others in the congregation, if not the parochial church council. Although you are not being officially ordained (we shall discuss this possibility later), a leader of a group often has to act for that group in its relationships with others, including the congregation. The approval of the clergy and the congregation, therefore, is essential if these relationships are to be established and maintained.

The Leader, the Group and the Congregation

When you lead a prayer group, you soon become aware of pressures being exerted on you — pressures to initiate, to check, to support, to oppose. It will be worth while examining these pressures briefly, for one of your problems will be to discern whether their source is the gentle prompting of God the Holy Spirit, or whether it is what we sum up in the catechism as "the world, the flesh and the devil".

You will sense these pressures coming into your consciousness from three different directions — from your inner self, from the members of the group, individually and corporately, and from outside the group, especially from the congregation.

It is nearly always difficult to discern at first the

source of pressures from within ourselves. Is the eagerness with which I am urging the group to adopt a project I have put before them motivated by God, or does it come from deep feelings of inadequacy which are driving me to try and control the group? Do I over-react against certain individuals in the group because I believe that they are misguided or because God is challenging me personally through what they say?

The more open you can be with the group about your inner self, the more you will find them helping you to discern the source of these inner pressures (and the more you will help them to be open about themselves). Of course, some matters cannot be shared with the group, especially if they are of a personal or confidential nature. These have to be left to the prayer and guidance of one or two close Christian friends. But many matters can be discussed in the group and, besides bringing a more powerful spirit of discernment, this helps to build up the group's confidence in you as their leader.

Generally speaking, if you know in your heart that you are trying to manipulate the group in some way, through calculated persuasion or feigned opposition, then it is likely that you are giving in to a pressure from within yourself — a fear, an ambition (the world, or the flesh, or the devil). But if you know that you are being open with the group in order to serve them in Christ's name, then you can be reasonably sure that the Holy Spirit will prompt what you do and say — and will work through you and them, in spite of your mistakes!

The pressure from the members of the group, individually and corporately, is constantly changing. Sometimes you will feel closer to certain individuals than to others. Then next week you will feel deserted by them. A suggestion from one individual will vividly reveal God's will to you. The same suggestion from another will sound like a criticism of your leadership. Personal animosities and prejudices cloud our discernment in relating to others.

Furthermore, as a leader you will find yourself engaged in a continual struggle to maintain a balance between giving everyone in the group freedom to say and to do what they wish, and checking one or all the members when that freeedom becomes disruptive. At one meeting they will act like responsible adults; at another it will seem to you as if they have all suddenly reverted to adolescent status in their behaviour.

Those discussions which threaten to reveal sharp differences of opinion are particularly difficult to handle. You fear that the group may be torn in two. There is a tendency in charismatic prayer groups to avoid discussions like these because they seem to break up the unity which everyone enjoys in the meetings. Yet it is a greater manifestation of the love of Christ when we can take up points of disagreement and allow the Holy Spirit to lead us through them. God's purposes are hardly ever established without a dialogue between those involved.

This is a leader's opportunity. In the discussion he can help both sides to feel unrestrained in expressing what they believe, and at the same time assist them in recognising the boundaries of Christian courtesy. Then members will begin to listen to one another and to seek the Spirit's guidance from what God is saying to them through their dialogue. It is true that the devil occasionally trips dialogue into dispute, causing disunity; but the leader can be like a watchman, issuing a warning when it seems as if this is about to happen, and assisting the group to return to a spirit of fellowship through patience and prayer.

The pressure from outside the group, especially from the congregation, is also constantly changing. Sometimes you will feel that the local Church is warmly supporting the group and your leadership. At other times they will seem critical, almost hostile. You will need the gift of God's wisdom in reacting to this pressure, for it is crucial that the unity of the Church, expressed through the relationships between the group and the congregation, is strengthened and built up through you as leader. Nothing serves the devil's devices more than stirring up factions until we get yet another Corinthian situation ("I belong to Paul" — "I belong to Apollos" — "I belong to Cephas") reproduced in our Christian fellowship.

For example, suppose your local parish church is mounting an evangelistic campaign. The parochial church council, acting through its committee for mission and unity, asks your group to visit the houses in the avenues where the members live. The request comes to you through the vicar, as chairman of the council and the committee.

What are you to do?

That will depend on the gift of discernment

that the Spirit gives you into the relationships between the group, the congregation, the vicar and yourself.

If those relationships are good — if you know that the group has confidence in the vicar, in the committee and in you — all you have to do is to tell him that you will ask the group at the next meeting if they will undertake the visiting.

But if those relationships are weak — if you suspect that a few members of the group are not in sympathy with the committee's plans, or if you believe that some will refuse to accept your lead when you make the suggestion to them — you will first have to think of ways in which the relationships can be strengthened before the proposal is put to the group. You might invite the vicar and/or a member of the committee to come to the group's next meeting so that the project can be discussed and prayed about together. It may well be that the group, having been informed of the strategy of the evangelistic campaign and having been shown how their visiting fits in with it, will be eager to join in the project.

This example is one tiny instance of the countless ways in which we share in Christ's ministry to his people. The text, "God was in Christ reconciling the world to himself" (I Corinthians 5: 19), is a scriptural foundation-stone on which the Church has built a doctrine of the atonement; but it is also a text for those who, under the guidance of the Spirit, are engaged in a continual ministry of reconciliation in Christ's name amid all the initiatives and rejections, proposals and criticisms, friendships and hostilities, which characterise the relationships between individuals and groups.

The charism of leadership is Christ in you as minister of reconciliation, enabling you to be the middleman in the midst of these pressures in the local Christian community. With the ordained leadership of the Church, you have to discern between the promptings of the Spirit and the promptings of those forces which are not of God. This is why the spiritual gift is so vital as the people of God move forward on that pilgrimage which takes them to the fulfilment of his will.

Enabler and Prophet

Regular meetings with your parish priest or minister (preferably with other leaders) facilitate this process of growing together as a group and as a congregation. The vicar and his group leaders form a subsidary prayer group whose task it is to maintain and strength relationships within the local Church. (I have discussed the possibilities for such a group in Chapter 9).

From the clergy and from others who are available in the wider Church (diocese, district, etc.) we can receive aid in learning leadership techniques and guidance in handling difficult pastoral problems.

Training is given to supplement the charism of leadership, not to distort it. Although God gives his gifts when and where he will, we have a responsibility to seek tuition to enable us to exercise our charism more fully.

Sensitivity training, now available through the education departments of the denominations, will teach us much as we seek to lead our groups from Bible study and prayer to ministry and mission.

We shall learn that different kinds of situations call for different kinds of leadership. A large assembly of people invariably requires a firm lead from the one presiding over it to keep it under control. The Speaker of the House of Commons has to act as a "dictator", making decisions about who shall be permitted to address the House and when a point of order is to be allowed. A clergyman conducting a service in church is in a similar position. This kind of leadership is called "dictatorial" — not because the leader is a political or ecclesiastical despot (though he *may* be that as well!) but because firm leadership is required if a large group of people are to achieve anything together. (Indeed, in a crowd many individuals need to know that someone is in control or they are gripped by a sense of terror that those around them may become aggressive — agitators and hooligans make use of these fears at political demonstrations and football matches.)

We shall also learn that in a small group leadership of a very different kind can be exercised, a "democratic" leadership which makes it possible for each member to participate in the group's life to the fullest extent. Individual initiative is encouraged. In these circumstances greater demands are made on the leader, for he is the one who enables the rest to participate and initiate. Since all the members of the Church are gifted by God for their ministry, it is this kind of group that gives most of them the maximum opportunity for discovering and exercising their charisms for the building up of the whole Church.

We need to understand the reasons for the tensions which spring up between one group and another. Inter-group exercises are a fascinating game which teach us much about relationships, not only between prayer groups and local congregations but also between the larger groups we meet everywhere in life.

As you get to know the members of your group, you will be more quick to respond to the Spirit's prompting: how to encourage shy individuals to enter more fully into the group's life, how to discern gifts in members and help them to exercise them, how to lead the group so that it faces up to problems and seeks God's solutions to them, and how to speak and act for the group when required.

You will be used by the Spirit to "steer" and to "give aid" as the group moves forward — one member contributing a word of wisdom in a discussion, another contributing a word of knowledge in a counselling session, another speaking in tongues, another interpreting or prophesying, another laying on hands for a gift of healing. Like the conductor of an orchestra, you will see and hear emerging under the baton of your leadership a new creative act of God's mercy in and through his Church.

Yet the best leaders are not only enablers: they are also prophets, men with a vision of Christ reigning gloriously over his Church and his world. Whatever training you do or do not receive, the charism of leadership will help you to share something of this vision with the rest of the group and encourage them to reach forward towards it.

You may feel hopelessly inadequate. Sometimes you will think that you made the biggest mistake of your life when you initiated a prayer group. Now and then you may want to run away from it.

But feelings are not our guide, only our faith; and God never deserts those whose faith is fixed in him. Indeed, it is as we believe that he accomplishes his work through us.

When the Holy Spirit overshadowed Mary for her unique charism of motherhood of God's Son, she acted out of faith, not out of feeling — and she was blessed by God, for it was through her faith that divine redemption came into the world:

"Blessed is she who *believed*, for there will be a fulfilment of what was spoken to her from the Lord" (Luke 1: 45 margin).

CHAPTER 3

Receiving God's Word

I SAID in the introduction that Christians gather into groups so that they may receive God's word. I was not implying that we cannot hear what God is saying to us in other ways — as, for example, when we meditate on the Bible and on his will for us privately. The daily quiet time has always been a vital means of inner communion with God. But because our salvation in Christ comes to us through the Church — through the Gospel of Jesus Christ proclaimed by the Church in the power of the Spirit — we never receive God's word in isolation from our experience of being one among many in the Christian family and beyond it.

Furthermore, our understanding of God's word has to be tested by the corporate understanding of the Church. And in sharing and testing our understanding with fellow Christians, our knowledge of the Father's purpose is enlightened and our faith in Jesus Christ, crucified and risen, is built up.

When the group has assembled, we settle down and read the chosen passage. There is a pause at the end and we try to let our minds freewheel under the momentum of the Holy Spirit. The silence may be prolonged as each member of the group turns a phrase or a text over in his mind, rather as a wine-taster will sip from the glass and roll the liquid over his tongue and against his palate. The pages of Bibles rustle as one or two look up references in the margins. Then someone makes a comment. Another follows, and the conversation begins. A wisp of humour warms the proceedings and helps to draw us together. A word of wisdom, given unexpectedly, is like a flash of light across a darkened sky. Slowly God unfolds for us the mystery of his will through the scriptures. We can say with the Psalmist, "Thy word is a lamp to my feet and a light to my path" (Psalm 119: 105).

Christians who are being renewed by the Spirit often say that the Bible has "come alive" for them in a new way. What has happened is that, being more aware of the Spirit as their Teacher they become more aware of the means by which he teaches them. The Spirit sharpens our hearing as we listen to the word of God. "He will glorify me," Christ told his disciples in the Fourth Gospel, "for he will take what is mine and declare it to you" (John 16: 14).

Thus the Spirit encourages us to listen to the scriptures with a renewed understanding and a living expectancy. As we reflect on a passage together in a group, familiar words and sentences sparkle with a relevance that we have never noticed before. Fresh and seemingly inexhaustible riches are unearthed from the books of the Old and the New Testaments, pointed out by one member and by another as we share our meditations. If the Spirit has control of a group of Christians pondering scripture together, the voice of the risen Christ can be clear indeed. Like the disciples we look back on the session with awe and joy: "Did not our hearts burn within us while he talked to us on the road, while he opened to us the scriptures?" (Luke 24: 32).

We want to raise questions, of course, and it is right that we should do so; but we must discriminate between questions which come from a reverent seeking after truth and those which come from an evil cynicism seeking to challenge that truth. For the word of God in scripture can be "living and active, sharper than any two-edged sword, piercing to the division of soul and spirit, of joints and marrow, and discerning the thoughts and intentions of the heart" (Hebrews 4: 12). When it pricks us personally we can take cover in the wrong kind of biblical criticism.

Let us, then, always approach our reflection on the Bible remembering that the Lord wants to speak to us. He wants to proclaim his love and his purpose from the rooftops of our understanding. If we find it difficult to hear what he is saying, it is because we are deafening his voice with our inattention, our doubts, or our unwillingness to accept what he knows is necessary for us at that particular moment. When we raise questions, we must ask them as those who humble themselves before God's word and who listen for the positive voice of Jesus Christ, knowing that "all the promises of God find their Yes in him" (I Corinthians 1: 20).

In our meditations we enter into a dialogue with the scriptures. On the one side of the dialogue are the scriptures themselves, the products of the old and the new Israel, written as "men moved by the Holy Spirit spoke from God" 2 Peter 1: 21). Since apostolic days, under the guidance of the same Spirit, the Church has recognised their authority as the primary source of God's revelation.

On the other side of the dialogue are ourselves, the products of our traditions and our culture. We bring to the dialogue what we have learned of God as he spoke to us through our inner response to him, through other Christians, through life itself. As the Creator Spirit, God speaks to us from this side of the dialogue as well.

No one, not even the most conservative fundamentalist, comes to the reading of the scriptures without entering that dialogue. He brings with him something of his own background, and because our backgrounds are so varied, we enter into the dialogue from different angles and levels. This is why in a mixed group of Christians the Bible *seems* to say different things to different people.

Since these differing backgrounds — our traditions and our cultures — are so important in our reflection on the Bible in the group, we must look at them for a moment.

Traditions and Cultures

Our traditions come from those schools of doctrine or forms of spirituality in which we have been brought up or into which we entered when we became members of the Church. The child of an Irish family in Liverpool will probably become a Roman Catholic; a man converted during a crusade organised by a Baptist church in a London suburb will probably become a Baptist. These factors look like accidents of social history, but because the Holy Spirit shows us that God is Lord of all history and of all society, we believe that factors like these are also within his purposes for those involved. In our prayer group, therefore, we must accept people as they are and not reject them because their starting-point in the dialogue with scripture is not the same as ours.

A consequence of this acceptance of one another is that God draws into groups Christians of different denominations. This development began through the ecumenical movement, but the charismatic renewal has accelerated it in recent years. Relationships between Christians of the various denominations has been transformed from polite neighbourliness to deep fellowship. Prayer groups that are both charismatic and ecumenical are perhaps one of the most notable signs of growing local Christian unity today.

But the differences created by traditions in doctrine, worship and discipline do not miraculously vanish when Christians are filled with the Spirit. Within an ecumenical prayer group tensions reappear when members' traditional outlooks conflict on matters like the remarriage of divorced people in church, the Roman Catholic discipline in mixed marriages, radical and conservative approaches to the Bible, admission to Communion, and so on.

Nor does growing together in the Spirit mean a renunciation of the traditions of our past. I still thank God for what I have experienced and learned as a result of being brought up in the Anglo-Catholic wing of the Church of England. Involvement in the charismatic renewal has illuminated still further much that was handed on to me through that great tradition.

We might say (echoing Paul) that by one Spirit we were all baptised into one body — Catholic or Protestant, radical or conservative, high Anglican or evangelical Anglican — and that when charismatics of differing traditions come together the Spirit shows them their basic unity in Jesus Christ first. After that, doctrinal, liturgical and disciplinary divergences are seen in a better perspective. The love of God which binds Christians together in the growing fellowship of a prayer group is so much greater than the things which separate us through our traditions. More aware of the Spirit's presence and power, we are more hopeful that he will one day lead us into a fuller unity.

I have experienced a little of this gentle process of being drawn closer to Christians of other traditions through prayer. In the Barnabas Fellowship at Whatcombe House God called together a group from widely divergent backgrounds. I shared in Bible reading and prayer with them every day for years. The daily encounter with the word of God was never easy, for in the course of our dialogue I was forced to re-examine ideas and practices which for years I had taken for granted as part of my Christian commitment. There were occasions when I felt the faith-stretching demands made on me were too much to bear, and I longed to escape back into the comparative security of my Anglo-Catholic bunker.

But in my heart I knew this was not God's will for me. The community's Bible reading and prayer times were moments when he seemed to be refining me in the purifying fire of the Spirit. Gradually, over the months, he gave us a deeper trust in one another, and our differences — though still real — became less important. What mattered was allowing a brother or a sister in Christ to respond to God as the Holy Spirit led him or her – through the tradition in which he or she had been brought up. And through that response, the dialogue was enriched for the rest of us.

Besides the differences in our traditions, the differences in our cultures also affect that dialogue. We can include under the title of "culture" everything in our experience that influenced our upbringing. Our differing Christian traditions may be part of our culture, but culture itself is wider than they are.

Some cultural differences are local, such as those between a man born and raised in a West Country middle-class home and one from an East London working-class family. Others are national, such as the difference between an English Christian and an

African or Asian believer. Yet other cultural differences are created or emphasised by our individual experience of life and the various kinds of education that are open to us.

Like differences in traditions, differences in cultures among the members of a prayer group can deepen our understanding of the word of God. One group I used to attend included among its members a woman who spent about six months each year in the Holy Land. Another group I knew included two West Indian Christians, newly arrived in England as immigrants. The contributions such people were able to make out of their experience was invaluable.

It is in the mixture of different cultures that the greater enlightenment of the Spirit is found, not in the dominance of one culture over another. A member of a group may have a university education or a diploma in theology, but this does not necessarily mean that the Lord will use him to unfold the divine wisdom in a group more than a less qualified member. Those of us who have had theological training need the assistance of others who, under the teaching of the Spirit, can approach scriptural passages and texts in a fresh, unacademic way. One of the most inspiring commentaries on the first chapters of Acts I ever heard was given by an Indian evangelist who has never read any book in his life except the Authorised Version of the Bible. No members of a group need ever feel shy of commenting on the scriptures because they think that the clergyman or the teacher of religious education who is present knows all that there is to know.

On the other hand, the group should respect the teaching office of the clergy and the specialised knowledge of the trained theologian. An anti-academic attitude can result in sectarian narrowness and intolerance. Belief in the gifts of the Spirit includes an acknowledgment that the charism of the teacher often comes through the normal channels of education.

I was once a member of a group which included a transport driver who had left school at an early age and a Roman Catholic Jesuit priest with high qualifications as a Biblical scholar. One evening, while we were discussing the problem of miracles, the driver said that he believed they were possible because a day rarely passed when he did not experience one. Pressed about this statement, he explained that as he was driving his delivery van through London, he often said a quick prayer when it looked as if his vehicle was about to be hit by a carelessly-driven car, and just as often it seemed as if his van was lifted on one side to avoid an accident.

Another member of the group took him up on this.

"Do you think God alters the laws of nature because you say a prayer?" he asked, with a hint of sarcasm in his voice.

"I know a lot about vehicles," said the driver, "but I can't account for what happens, laws of nature or not."

Then the Jesuit spoke.

"Who are we to tell God what are the laws of nature?" he asked quietly.

There was a long pause. The Holy Spirit had used

both the unacademic driver and the trained theologican to reveal a little more of the mystery of God's ways with man.

Moving Together

Although it is the leader's task to ensure that all the members of a group have an opportunity to share in the reflective reading of the Bible, we can each facilitate this by putting the others first, urging them to make a contribution before we do, welcoming what they say and giving it careful attention. The injunctions of Paul have a special relevance: "There must be no room for rivalry and personal vanity among you, but you must humbly reckon others better than yourselves. Look to each other's interest and not merely to your own" (Philippians 2 : 3–4).

Yet disagreements do sometimes arise. We find ourselves rejecting the views of another in the group. What he says seems to us so unreasonable, so contrary to everything we have ever believed, that we feel rising within us what we take as a righteousness determination to refute what he is saying.

The fierceness of our reactions should be its own warning. "In quietness and peace shall be your strength" (Isaiah 30: 15). As we feel the surge of opposition rising within us, we must ask ourselves why the other's views are affecting us in this way. Am I being used by the Spirit in the dialogic search for truth or am I opposing him because what he said has aroused a fear in me — a sure sign that my security is being threatened? When we have asked these questions, we can then go on to ask others. What is the Lord saying to me through the views that I find so difficult to accept? What is the Spirit teaching me through the tension I feel?

Or perhaps we are in a group where a dispute is rising between two of the members. We shall be acting irresponsibly if we mentally sit back and watch the dispute develop. We are part of the dispute because we are united in Christ with the participants. So we can ask God in a quiet prayer to re-establish his peace among us and look for an opportunity to be used as his agent in answering that prayer. Perhaps we can help the disputants to clarify their ideas, or suggest that the views being put forward are not so distant as they appear to be. Unless one of the disputants is obviously in the wrong, we should avoid taking sides. "A gentle tongue is a tree of life" (Proverbs 15:4). Every group needs that kind of wisdom.

There is nothing "uncharismatic" about disagreements. Unity is not forced on us by the Spirit. It is the goal towards which he urges us as we move nearer to God in Jesus Christ. The author of Ephesians saw Christian discipleship as a continuing progress: "In him you ... *are being built* with all the rest into a spiritual dwelling for God" (Ephesians 2:22, my italics). We can expect differences to persist until God's people are perfected in the kingdom of Heaven. What would be uncharismatic would be to reject other Christians because of their views.

However, expressions of disagreement are not always signs of divergent ideas. They can also be symptomatic of people's needs. A member of a group has problems at his place of employment and his anxiety shows itself in an argument about a scriptural text. A couple are worried about their teenage son and their fears manifest themselves in endless nagging about some point of doctrine. Their needs have to be met, not with carefully expressed views but with concern and prayer.

But in a group which is open to the Spirit we shall avoid these problems for most of the time. Instead, we experience the word of God as the creator and sustainer of our Christian fellowship. We begin to look forward to each meeting of the prayer group as a time when our minds and spirits are fed by the scriptures. We become conscious of a deep yearning to know more of God through Jesus Christ. Jesus said, "I am the bread of life; he who comes to me shall not hunger, and he who believes in me shall never thirst" (John 6: 35). We realise why the Church has never interpreted the discourse in the sixth chapter of the Fourth Gospel solely in sacramental terms.

Practicalities

Each group must decide for itself how it sets about its Bible reading, what passages it selects and how it discusses them. We can begin by looking at the lectionary in use in our local church and choose for our reading one of the passages set for the following Sunday. Then we shall "hear" the ministry of the word in church more profitably. Indeed, if the parish priest or minister is a member of the group, his sermon may well evolve out of the discussion. Or we can devise our own scheme, reading through a book, or part of a book, varying this by turning to a set theme (such as the promises of Christ or the New Testament teaching on the Church), looking up the various passages related to it after consulting one of the many biblical guides that are available.

In the initial stages the members of a new group may require assistance in approaching the scriptures together. Bible reading techniques abound. A simple one is to give each member in the group a piece of paper divided by lines into three sections. On the left-hand side of the top section is a question mark, of the middle section an exclamation mark, and of the bottom section a tiny sketch of a candle. The passage is read aloud and the group is asked to spend a few minutes thinking about it. During this time they make notes on the paper of things that come into their minds — problems connected with the passages in the top section (the question mark), things that strike them forcibly in the middle section (the exclamation mark), and matters on which they have received enlightenment in the bottom section (the candle). After the silence the leader gives each member two minutes to read out or to comment on his notes before opening the passage to general discussion.

The advantage of techniques such as this is that everyone is encouraged to participate and share in their reflections. After a few meetings techniques are not so necessary as the members of the group get to know one another and become experienced enough to contribute their thoughts freely.

Occasionally we can set the Bible aside for a few weeks and read another book together. Spiritual classics such as Julian of Norwich's *Revelations of Divine Love* or modern works like Arthur Wallis's *Pray in the Spirit* help us to hear the word of God as he speaks through the life and experiences of his people. We are also made aware of the oneness of the Spirit's fellowship across the centuries.

After selecting a title, each member buys or borrows a copy. One of us prepares by reading a chapter and introducing it at the next meeting — summarising its substance if it is long and reading aloud a few key paragraphs.

Then we must listen to the voice of God in the midst of his world. Newspapers, journals, radio and TV saturate us with news and views and sensationalism blunts our discernment, but God still says to us, as he said to the prophet, "Amos, what do you see?" Prophecy is more than inspired utterance: it is the Spirit's gift to see the finger of God pointing in the midst of local, national and international events.

Yet in our groups we shall always return to the Bible, for it provides the measure against which all else is appraised. Without the scriptures we shall not discern fully what God is saying through other books and doing through contemporary events.

And since many Christians in the current renewal movement are experiencing the charisms of prophecy and interpretation, it is all the more necessary that what they hear should be tested by the teaching of the sacred writings. Enthusiasm can all too easily drift into error. In the resurgence of Christian awakening there is always an unhappy tendency for some to "turn away from listening to the truth and wander into myths" 2 Timothy 4 : 4). In the last analysis, the criterion of all true prophecy is its accord with known revelation.

CHAPTER 4

Praying Together

RECEIVING GOD'S word through reflection on the scriptures, the Church and the world, the group begins its response to him in prayer.

I would not like to have to explain precisely where one activity ceased and the other commenced! We continue to receive God's word as we pray, and thoughts about the scriptures, the Church and the world crowd into our penitence, our intercessions and our praises. For the purposes of this book, however, I will say that prayer begins when the group stops its meditative conversation arising from the Bible and focuses its attention directly on God's presence. Christ taught his disciples, "When you pray, say: Father, hallowed be thy name" (Luke 11 : 2). We will assume, then, that the group begins its prayer when it addresses God.

We soon realise, if we have not realised it before, that there is nothing in our lives which cannot be the topic of prayer. "Have no anxiety about anything, but in everything by prayer and supplication with thanksgiving, let your requests be made known to God" (Philippians 4: 6). We notice how Paul and the other New Testament writers constantly urged their readers to pray, and in Acts the outpouring of the Spirit resulted in prayers from the apostolic Church. In the current wave of renewal in the Churches, many are re-discovering the joy and strength which the Spirit gives to God's people when they pray together.

Behind this experience is the theological truth that no prayer is really *my* prayer or *our* prayer: it is always *God's* prayer. For God is not the object of our praying, since prayer is not just thoughts and words addressed to him. Rather, he is the subject of our praying, because when we pray we allow the Holy Spirit to move through us, our mind, our spirit, our whole personality, drawing us in love towards the Father.

To pray together, then, is to be joined in a spiritual pilgrimage in Christ which ends at the throne of God in heaven. We become vehicles of the Spirit; he takes our thoughts, our hopes, our fears, our imaginings, the promptings that stem from the deepest levels of our personalities, and purifies them and unites them with his on-going, eternal relationship with the Father through the Son. "When we cry, 'Abba! Father!' it is the Spirit himself bearing with our spirit that we are children of God" (Romans 8: 15–16). That is why formal, liturgical prayer ends with the ascription, "Through Jesus Christ our Lord who with thee, Father, and the Holy Spirit, art ever one God, world without end."

In prayer our feelings are secondary — as in any Christian activity. If we feel we want to pray together, that is good, for it gives us an added incentive; but it is not the main reason why we pray. We pray in a group because we believe that this is what the Lord wants us to do whether we happen to feel like it or not. The members who do not feel like praying at a particular meeting can be helped by the will to pray which the others have.

"Prayer is the deliberate act of the soul," wrote Julian of Norwich. "It is true, full of grace, and lasting, for it is united with and fixed into the will of our Lord by the inner working of the Holy Spirit."*

The leader can assist the group to respond to God in prayer by encouraging a relaxed yet reverent atmosphere through his own attitude. In this atmosphere members will gradually feel that they can share their joys or their anxieties spontaneously — one of the healing and strengthening purposes of coming together in the Spirit.

The leader must beware of trying to work up a spirit of devotion by the use of choruses and suchlike. When choruses are used, it should be because their words provide a fitting means through which a group can express itself in response to God. Otherwise the singing will create an artificial atmosphere which is repulsive to many.

Perhaps after a few intercessions, there is a long pause, broken when one member of the group is

* *Revelations of Divine Love*, c. 41 (ed. C. Wolters, Penguin Books, p. 124.)

moved to utter expressions of praise. These are continued when another begins a verse from a hymn or a chorus which, though familiar to us, amazes us with its aptness and freshness. A passage from scripture is read out as a further act of praise. Exclamations of wonder come from the group. Then the silence overshadows us again until more words are spoken — a few sentences, perhaps a simple prophecy — which we discern as an insight into the mind of God himself. Our openness to God is allowing him to be free with us.

"He wants to be free to think through our minds, feel through our hearts, speak through our lips, and even weep through our eyes and groan through our spirits. When the believer is thus at the disposal of the Holy Spirit, praying in the Spirit will be a reality."*

As the weeks go by we become more sensitive to the promptings in others and in ourselves. We learn to test when we are being moved by the Spirit. Our instinctive reactions come under closer scrutiny. Instead of blurting out the first thing that comes into our heads, we become more poised in attention upon God, speaking only when we are sure he wants us to contribute. We respond warmly to another's need; we are less self-justifying in what we say ourselves. We ask God to take away critical thoughts that arise when someone else is praying; we grow in trust and love as the Spirit brings us together in the body of Christ. God, we slowly discover, brings his own order into our apparent spontaneity, and the advice that

* Arthur Wallis, *Pray in the Spirit* (Victory Press, 1970), p. 22

Paul gave to the Christians in Corinth takes on a new meaning:

> When you come together, each one has a hymn, a lesson, a revelation, a tongue, or an interpretation. Let all things be done for edification. If any speak in a tongue, let there be only two or at most three, and each in turn; and let one interpret. But if there is no one to interpret, let each of them keep silence in church and speak to himself and to God. Let two or three prophets speak, and let the others weigh what is said. If a revelation is made to another sitting by, let the first be silent. For you can all prophesy one by one, so that all may learn and all be encouraged; and the spirits of prophets are subject to prophets. For God is not a God of confusion but of peace (I Corinthians 14: 26–33).

Early Problems

Two early problems encountered by people in groups when they begin to pray together for the first time might be labelled "the problem of the sound barrier" and "the problem of the verbal flood".

The problem of the sound barrier is an inability to address God directly aloud in prayer when others are listening. There are devout Christians who enjoy church services, discuss their faith and pray inwardly for long periods. But ask them to offer an intercession or an act of praise in the prayer group and you might as well invite them to leap over a high wall. They are tongue-tied.

For a few of them it may be a matter of faith. To speak to an invisible Person in the presence of others is not easy for those whose doubts trouble them. They feel there is something fundamentally dishonest in it — for them. Baptism in the Holy Spirit requires faith in Jesus Christ as Saviour, and an experience of spiritual renewal will sometimes overcome this problem, especially if the person concerned is given the charism of tongues. But even after an experience like that, one or two still have to be helped before they can join in spontaneous prayer.

For a few others it may be simply a matter of custom. Anglicans in particular are so used to listening to prayers said for them in church that they find it difficult to begin to pray aloud with others for themselves.

And for the rest — and they are probably the majority — it may just be a case of modesty and shyness. Shall I say the right thing? they ask themselves. What will the rest of the group think of me if I make a grammatical error in the prayer or utter an unacceptable heresy?

God usually provides opportunities for these hesitant ones to be freed. In one group a woman — I will call her Mary — had this difficulty. She had been bought up in an Anglo-Catholic parish and for her spontaneous prayer was strange and outlandish. She had thought only Free Churchmen indulged in it!

"I just feel as if there's a great gag wrapped round me," she explained to the group.

We expressed our sympathy, and this encouraged her to go on to admit that she and her husband had never been able to pray openly together at home. They had often knelt down by their bedside at night and said their prayers privately, but they had never done this aloud.

At that meeting we had been discussing the responsibilities of Christion parents and telling each other the effect our own fathers and mothers had had on our religious upbringing. When we began to pray, it seemed as if the Lord suddenly gave me an idea that would help Mary out of her difficulty.

I suggested that we each in turn thanked God as our heavenly Father for all that our parents had meant to us in bringing us to a knowledge of his love for us in Christ. (Although some of the group had had non-practising Christians as parents, I knew that they had seen God's loving care in their fathers and mothers.) I added that if anyone could not think of what to say, they might mention the names of their parents and say, "Glory be to the Father . . ."

Then I spoke the name of each person in the group, trying to sound as relaxed and casual as I could.

"Robert, would you care to begin?"

He thanked God for his father's discipline; although he had resented it when he was younger, he realised that it had done much to help him develop a logical and tidy mind.

"Now you, Ruth."

She praised God for the welcoming atmosphere she had always found in her parents' home; she told God she believed his heavenly home would be like that.

"And you, Mary."

There was a short pause. I could not resist the temptation to open an eye and look at her. She appeared to be bracing herself, as if preparing to dive into cold water!

Then, with astonishing fluency and grace, she said a short prayer for her parents.

She gasped with delight.

"It — just — came!" she exclaimed.

We all laughed. Mary had broken her sound barrier.

That night, when she went home, she prayed spontaneously with her husband for the first time in their married life.

The incident taught me that it is usually easier for people to break through the sound barrier in prayer when they are praising and thanking God for those they love rather than when they are interceding for them. To intercede you have to think about the ones you are praying for and formulate suitable words and phrases on their behalf. To praise and thank God for them you simply look at the Lord and use any words and phrases that come into your mind.

The problem of the verbal flood often stems from causes similar to those that create the problem of the sound barrier in people. Lacking faith, a man prays at length to convince himself (and perhaps others) that God does exist and can hear, supporting himself in flights of rhetorical encouragement. Nervousness can so grip another that once he has started speaking he finds it difficult to stop (young ordination candidates suffer from this in their sermons). The

Free Churches tolerated long extemporary prayers until quite recently. (I have experienced one such prayer that went on for twenty minutes *after* I had looked impatiently at my watch!)

One group dealt with this problem in a tactful and successful manner. The man who prayed at length was approached privately by a friend who suggested that when this happened again, he (the friend) would deliberately interrupt the talker, either by taking up the prayer or by cutting it short with some remark. The member agreed. The friend only had to do this once or twice during further meetings before the member mastered himself. He afterwards told his friend that when the interruption came, it was as if a heavy burden had been lifted from his shoulders.

Penitence

For those who imagine that devotions in charismatic prayer groups are all praise and glory, it is a shock to learn that penitence for our personal sins can be the deepest form of prayer that we experience in some meetings. This is because when the Spirit of God comes to us, he brings more than gifts; he also brings a piercing light into our failings. "When he comes, he will convict the world of sin" (John 16: 8). In his light we see more clearly that which is evil and unbelieving in our hearts. But with the light he also brings the cleansing power of God. John the Baptist announced Christ as the one who baptises "with the Holy Spirit and with fire" (Matthew 3: 11, Luke 3: 16), "fire" being symbolic of the purifying work of God.

Penitence is not expressed at every meeting, nor is it right that it should be, but occasionally one of the members in the group will be moved to ask God for forgiveness for a specified or unspecified fault — it could be a matter which has been aired in the reflection on the Bible — and this will lead the others to declare their own repentance.

We become aware of the effects of sin on our relationships with others in the Church — the ecclesial dimension of sin, as the theologians call it. We see that sin is not only a breach between ourselves and God; it is also a weakening of the body of Christ. Jesus taught that reconciliation with one another was necessary before we could be forgiven by God. Paul said that a member of the Church guilty of a grave sin was like leaven in the ritual passover bread: it made the bread unfit for cultic purposes.

The fellowship of a group is wonderfully strengthened when a disagreement leading to a clash between two of its members is reconciled during a meeting, both apologising to one another and then offering their mutual reconciliation to God in prayer. It is not uncommon for individuals to be moved to tears — and we learn that references in the scriptures to weeping for sin are not as extravagant as we once assumed. As one who goes to confession before the greater festivals of the Church, I have to say that while the absolution pronounced by the priest gives an assurance of forgiveness through the sacramental means of grace, the prayers of a group after my admission of a fault are equally assuring of God's forgiveness.

There are, of course, risks. Certain sins ought not to be confessed in public, not even in an intimate prayer group. The injunction, "Confess your faults to one another" (James 5:16), has never been interpreted as permission for an unrestrained acknowledgment of personal failings. The Church has condemned this practice from earliest times and ensured that confessions made to the clergy are protected by the seal of the confessional. If there is someone in the group whose exhibitionist tendencies, or sense of condemnation, leads them beyond the bounds of what may wisely be confessed, the leader or another member should suggest that this is a matter for private counselling after the meeting.

Many of us have found the grace of God through asking others in the group to pray for us when facing particular temptations and difficulties. The sense of loneliness in the midst of our problems, which is one of the biggest burdens many Christians have to bear, is driven away if we can share them with a group. Needless to say, it is only as the members of the group feel they can trust one another that they can help one another in this way. Trust grows as individual members commit themselves to group. Occasionally they may be disappointed and perhaps hurt, but it is only through disappointments and hurts that the trust of a group can be tested.

After spontaneous acts of penitence, it is wise to anchor the prayer in a well-known formulary of the Church. One of the penitential psalms can be recited by the group from their Bibles (e.g., Psalms 6, 32, 51, 130, 143). Or they can join in a form of general confession, such as that printed in the Church of England's *Series Three Order for Holy Communion*.

At a time when the formal fast before receiving Communion has practically disappeared, the charismatic renewal is recalling many to this discipline. When accepted in humility fasting can be an aid to our prayers; it seems as if the deliberate renunciation of a basic human desire for half-a-day, a whole day, or longer, sharpens our devotion along with the conscious denial of self that mounting hunger proclaims. Groups may encourage their members to accept the discipline together when praying for specific needs, but only in the spirit of Christ's injunction, "When you fast, anoint your head and wash your face, that your fasting may not be seen by men but by your Father who is in secret" (Matthew 6: 17).

Intercession

The intention of all prayer, including intercession for ourselves and for others, is that God may be glorified in Jesus Christ. Ultimately our petition that somebody may be aided through a problem or that somebody else may be healed is not offered only that the problem may be solved or health restored: it is offered that through the solution or the healing the power and majesty of God may be recognised by men. "Whatever you ask in my name, I will do it, that the Father may be glorified in the Son" (John 14 : 13). This text provides the course by which we set our mental compasses when we pray.

Charismatic prayer groups are rediscovering the

value of positive prayer. Seizing the promises of Christ made in texts like the one just quoted, they intercede with a new confidence. "Lord, we ask you, knowing that you have said . . ."

This is faith-building, for there is little point in praying unless we believe God can act. Yet in the midst of our confident calls upon the mercy and power of God to change people and situations, we must never lose our reverence for the mystery of God's ultimate purposes for ourselves and for his world. Even with the illumination that the Spirit brings, we still only see through a glass darkly, and this reverence should prompt us to pray always with deep humility.

Arrogance can creep into the intercessions of charismatic prayer groups. Then they address the Holy Spirit as if he were a faithful sheepdog, rushing hither and thither to comply with their biddings. "There is a time to keep silence, and a time to speak" (Ecclesiastes 3: 7). There is a time when, after careful reflection and discernment, the confident assertion of our belief that God will act in a certain way can be expressed in our prayers; there are other times when true wisdom prompts us to acknowledge our ignorance by silence.

It is worth while remembering that "in the days of his flesh, Jesus offered up prayers and supplications, with loud cries and tears, to him who was able to save him from death, and he was heard for his godly fear" (Hebrews 5: 7). Even so, Christ once explained that he did not know his Father's will about a particular subject (Mark 13: 32) and on the night of his betrayal he asked to be delivered from death (Mark 14: 36, John 18: 11). That request was refused. "Although he was a Son, he learned obedience through what he suffered; and being made perfect he became the source of eternal salvation to all who obey him" (Hebrews 5: 8). We intercede for others that they may share in this source of salvation by being obedient as Christ was.

So true intercession requires preparation, sensitivity and discernment. If our petitions are to reach the deeper purposes of God for individuals and events, we shall have to concentrate on a few at a time. This is why a basic guideline for intercession is: to be effective, be selective. We need to "pray through" the subjects we select. Behind the parables of the friend at midnight and the unjust judge (Luke 11: 5–8; 18: 1–5) is the encouragement to persist in petitionary prayer — not, as it were, to persuade God to change his mind, but to demonstrate the reality of our concern. A relationship between a married couple is breaking down, a member of the group is facing a personal crisis at his place of employment, another member's parent is critically ill — these are the kind of topics that invite a special concern during the prayers at their meetings.

The strength of a group at prayer lies in the fact that different members discern in different ways. A mixed group is particularly valuable for this reason. Women have an insight which complements the discernment of men; similarly, men have a detachment and pragmatism which helps to balance the emotional reactions of women. After an accident involving a neighbour's child, Mary's prayer lifted up the anguish of the parents sitting at the hospital bedside while life was endangered. As a mother, she saw the accident from the parents' viewpoint. It was left to another in the group to pray for the driver, who might be suffering the bitterness of self-accusation in the midst of his explanations that it was the child's fault.

Praise

Penitence and intercession are the forecourts of the temple of prayer. With praise we enter the sanctury. The people in Jerusalem on the day of Pentecost heard the Spirit-filled disciples telling of God's mighty works, and praise was the theme of the apostolic Church's prayer when threatened with persecution. In the midst of all their other concerns, the letters of the New Testament are full of expressions of praise. "Whatever you do, in word or deed," wrote Paul, "do everything in the name of the Lord Jesus, giving thanks to God the Father through him" (Colossians 3: 17).

Praise, then, is the fullest response of the people whom God has saved through Jesus Christ and filled with his Spirit. Our Lord told his disciples that their sorrow would be turned into joy at his resurrection and the sending of the Spirit: "I will see you again and your hearts will rejoice, and no one will take your joy from you" (John 16: 22). Joy is one of the fruits of the Spirit and praise is its expression on our lips.

It is a pity that charismatics tend to use too carelessly the acclamation, "Praise the Lord!" some make a habit of saying it with every other sentence they utter. (I have a friend who did this until I started calling her "Alleluia Edna"!) The magnificent phrase becomes ridiculous when thoughtlessly spoken.

We offer our praises to God when the Spirit leads us into that state of thankfulness in which other prayers would be inappropriate. We turn our eyes away from ourselves and towards him. We do not have to consider our own failings and we do not have to dwell on our own or other peoples' problems. We are conscious of our foothold in eternity. Each member of the group exults in God as Creator, Redeemer and Sanctifier. Baptised in the water of the Spirit, our whole being is lifted up towards God in thanksgiving: "I give water in the wilderness, rivers in the desert, to give drink to my chosen people, the people whom I have formed for myself, that they might declare my praise" (Isaiah 43: 20–21).

But we can also offer our praises when there is a feeling of depression during a meeting. Thanksgiving is a powerful antidote to gloom. Perhaps we begin to sing a chorus softly, or to recite a psalm. Slowly the others join in. The heaviness is lifted.

The psalmist discovered this secret. He began:

"I am poor and needy:
and my heart is disquieted within me . . ."

But he went on:

"I will give thanks to the Lord with my mouth:
and praise him among the multitude"

(Psalm 109: 22, 29)

Words and phrases from the scripture passage that the group has been reading can be woven into our praises and thanksgivings. We can recall the works of God which have been revealed to us, linking them with the signs of divine grace in our own lives. The eucharistic prayers of the Church, such as The Thanksgiving in the Church of England's *Series Three Order for Holy Communion,* provide us with a pattern round which we can build our own spontaneous praises. A feature of the preface of that prayer is that it dwells on the creative, redemptive and sanctifying work of God until it reaches a climax in the angelic song, "Holy, Holy, Holy Lord".

I once noted down a prayer of thanksgiving uttered in a prayer group by a woman who, I am sure, had never deliberately studied the structure of these eucharistic formulas:

Blessed be my heavenly Father, who created me and all men and everything that is good, for himself in all eternity.

Blessed be Jesus Christ, his Son and our Saviour, who died on the cross and rose again, and who lifts me and all God's children to a royal inheritance in glory.

Blessed be the Holy Spirit of God, who fills me with love for himself and for all his children, and who strengthens me, that Jesus may be glorified.

The Spirit, who has inspired the eucharistic prayers of the Church across the centuries, put on to the lips of this woman a thanksgiving of the same pattern. It was to me a wonderful demonstration of the time-lessness of praise as it rises from God's people.

The litany form also provides a pattern of praise. The leader or a member of the group invokes Jesus Christ by proclaiming his titles, and the rest repeat a suitable response:

"You are the Good Shepherd" — "We praise you, Lord of glory."

"You are the Lamb of God" — "We praise you, Lord of glory."

"You are the Saviour" — "We praise you, Lord of glory." And so on . . .

Praise can lead to silence, when the glory of God seems to shine in the hearts and minds of everyone in the group, uniting them in speechless adoration. Classical spirituality calls this experience the state of contemplation — the direct awareness of the presence of God in which verbal communication is superfluous.

During such moments we only want to utter, softly under our breath, the precious name of Jesus.

CHAPTER 5

Ministering to one another

So FAR in this book we have discussed the formation and leadership of the charismatic prayer group, its reception of the word of God, and its response in penitence, intercession and praise. Now we must go on to consider the group's response to the word of God in the practical matter of meeting human need. For the group that concerns itself only with Bible reading and prayer is hardly Christian and certainly not charismatic! Our thanksgiving to God must lead us to share in the ministry of Jesus Christ to his people and to the world.

But what do we mean by "ministry"?

Diakonia, like *koinonia*, is another famous word in scriptural vocabulary. To the Greek of the first century A.D. it signified the duties of a slave — holding the basin in which hands were washed, offering the towel, waiting at table, pouring out the wine. The distinction between a master and his servant was nowhere more apparent than at meals, when the noblemen reclined at low tables in long robes while the slaves, with their clothes girded, attended to their wants. We find the word used in its original sense in New Testament texts such as, "Prepare supper for me, and gird yourself and serve me" (Luke 17:8) and, "Martha served" (John 12:2).

The advantage of the word from an etymological viewpoint was that it did not suggest the kind of political or ecclesiastical service involving honour or authority. This is probably why Jesus coined it to describe the service which he himself offered and which he expected his disciples to offer. He answered their debate about precedence by saying, "Let the greatest among you become as the youngest, and the leader as one who serves. For which is the greater, one who sits at table, or one who serves? Is it not the one who sits at table? But I am among you as one who serves" (Luke 22:26–27).

To the notion of slave-like service, therefore, Christ brought a radically new meaning: he demonstrated in his life and self-offering that to serve, to "deacon", is to love one's neighbour in such a way that the love of God is manifested. It is more than the devoted attention of a faithful slave; it is to enter into and share in the service of the Servant of God for men.

But the attitude of the Christian who serves must be correctly understood. It is not just an overflowing generosity towards those in need, the hungry, the thirsty, the stranger, the naked, the poor and the imprisoned. Nor is it a form of self-abasement which robs the Christian of the dignity of his manhood.

Rather, it is the attitude of one who, knowing he is saved by Christ and filled with the Spirit of God, makes himself available for others and commits himself to them in the way Jesus Christ committed himself to man in obedience to the Father.

Now "ministry" and "to minister" are frequently used to translate *diakonia* and its associated verb, *diakoneo*. The impact of the word is partially muffled by the fact that we use it in a specialised manner to designate the Church's pastors — the "ordained Ministry". This leaves the impression that "ministering" is the exclusive concern of the clergy. Yet the New Testament, while it recognises the importance of authorised ministers chosen from among the congregation and ordained by prayer and the laying on of hands, nevertheless teaches that the work of ministry is that to which every Christian is called by being one with Christ. The special ministry of the pastor is but a sign of the total ministry of Christ in which every member of the Church is invited to share.

We are shown through the New Testament how widespread and yet how simple this ministry can be. Anything that one Christian does for someone else in the name of Jesus is a ministry — the collection and handing out of monies for the poor brethren in Jerusalem (2 Corinthians 8: 1–6, &c.), the personal help given to Paul by Timothy and Erastus (Acts 19: 22), Onesimus' service to Paul in prison on Philemon's behalf (Philemon 13), Onesiphorus' activities at Ephesus (2 Timothy 1: 18), the general expressions of love in action among Christians (1 Corinthians 16: 15, Hebrews 6: 10, Revelation 2: 19).

This is the real purpose of spiritual gifts. *Charismata* are for others, not for those who manifest them. Gifts and ministries are, therefore, intimately related. Every ministry is a manifestation of a spiritual gift. In the proper sense of the word, to be "charismatic" is to respond to God's call to participate in the ministry of Christ and to receive from him the gifts of the Spirit required in responding to that call — to be, in fact, a Christian!

Gifts and Ministries

What kinds of ministry can we offer one another in a prayer group?

I think it is sensible to begin with ordinary acts of neighbourly assistance. In charismatic circles it is easy to assume that the Holy Spirit equips us to minister to one another through the more remarkable charisms, forgetting that commonplace gifts are just as necessary in every day life. The apostle listed "service", "he who contributes" and "he who does acts of mercy" alongside praying and prophesying in his catalogue of spiritual gifts (Romans 12: 6–8). Contributing to the needs of the saints and practising hospitality today expresses itself in practical help during a domestic crisis, assistance when a difficult do-it-yourself task has to be completed, and baby-sitting so that a couple can go out to celebrate a wedding anniversary. Take any group of people in a city or a country area and it is not long before simple needs like these emerge providing opportunities for ministry.

For many Christians this is where their ministry ends. They will gladly offer themselves for practical acts of kindness. When I was vicar of a parish, I was often encouraged by the willingness of individual members of the congregation to tackle all kinds of jobs on behalf of their neighbours and the local church. They would baby-sit, decorate the church property, give lifts to the elderly, deliver and collect Christian Aid envelopes, with little thought of the personal inconvenience involved. But ask them to pray with the couple for whose baby they cared one evening, or suggest that they might be guided by God to lay hands on the sick person to whom they took a parcel of garden produce from the church's harvest festival, and they would be startled. "What? Me, vicar? I couldn't do that!"

Now ordinary parishioners *are* doing those things — plus other acts of ministry that they would never have thought of before. As the Holy Spirit enters their lives more powerfully, they realise that ministry of this kind is part of normal Christian discipleship. Through their involvement with charismatic prayer groups, meetings and conferences, they are learning that spiritual gifts are bestowed by God widely and freely among his people for his purposes and that, if they offer themselves to him, he will use them as his instruments in ministry. They accept for themselves passages such as this from the New Testament:

"As each has received a gift, employ it for one another, as good stewards of God's varied grace: whoever speaks, as one who utters oracles of God;

whoever renders service, as one who renders it by the strength which God supplies; in order that in everything God may be glorified through Jesus Christ" (I Peter 4: 10–11).*

In a prayer group where we know that we are accepted and trusted, we shall be willing to experiment — to take risks, even — in ministry to others. We shall dare to use our tongue aloud and wait for an interpretation. We shall launch into an interpretation ourselves when someone else speaks in a tongue. We shall use our imagination in uttering simple prophecies or in describing inspired pictures. We would never have the nerve to do anything like that at a formal Christian gathering (at Evensong in church, for instance!) but we can seek spiritual gifts in a group because we know that they will pardon our mistakes. If the "prophecy" meant nothing to anyone, no harm has been done. We can try again sometime, endeavouring to understand more clearly what God wills to say through us.

And we can be encouraged personally when we are used by God in ministry in a group. To speak in tongues and to hear afterwards that a member was assisted in a powerful way, or to lay hands on a member suffering from asthma and to be rung up next day and told that no trace of it bothered her

* The R.S.V.'s use of *as* could be a little misleading (and no other modern version I have looked at makes it clearer). "As one who utters oracles of God" and "As one who renders it by the strength which God supplies" means "Speak in such a way that your words *are* oracles of God" and "Serve in such a way that your activities *are* works of God." It is God who inspires "both the will and the deed" (Philippians 2:13).

during the night — incidents such as these make it worth while to experiment and to take risks.

Having seen God glorified through one spiritual gift, we are more open to the possibility that he may be glorified through another.

A friend wrote to me: "I've come to realise how much speaking in tongues helps me in talking to others. Every time I speak in tongues I have to commit my voice to the Lord and trust him to reveal his will through an interpretation. When other people are telling me about their problems, or when I have to speak to others about Jesus, I find I can give my voice to him in the same way and let him form the words and the sentences for me."

It is because the charisms enable us to participate in the ministry of Christ to others that we are to "earnestly desire the higher gifts". It is a pity that Paul's advice comes in the last verse of chapter twelve of 1 Corinthians, for that artificial division tends to separate it from the subsequent verses at the beginning of chapter thirteen. The "more excellent way" which the apostle draws is that thirteenth chapter — the way of love, faith, hope and joy — is the way of Christ's ministry in which we share as we seek to receive higher charisms from God.

But it is in humility that we receive more from God, and this is why one of the best means of learning to minister to others is to be willing to be ministered to ourselves. To suggest — if only by implication — that renewal in the Spirit sweeps aside all personal difficulties and disappointments is to run the risk of falling into pride; to pose as one without problems or

temptations is to erect an icy barrier between ourselves and the rest of the group.

Our difficulties may not be very great, but we can
strengthen the fellowship of the Spirit by sharing
them with the group. This will encourage others,
perhaps with greater problems than ours, to do the
same. Out of this sharing in ministry comes the grace
of Jesus Christ, and we experience the reality behind
Paul's assurance that "in all these things we are more
than conquerors through him who loved us"
(Romans 8: 37).

Counselling

The charismatic prayer group ministers together
when it listens to the personal problems of a member
and supports him or her through prayer and counselling.

With experience the group will learn how to be
guided corporately by the Spirit. Sometimes the lead
in counselling and praying will be taken by one particular member because the rest of the group sense
that he is the one among them whom God is going to
use in this case. Sometimes the lead will be shared,
one member speaking gently after another. Provided
the group is sensitive to the Spirit and to the reactions
in the one being prayed for and counselled, the love
of God will be revealed through the body of Christ
manifested in that group. This form of joint ministry
is usually called "body ministry". In it, different
members exercise similar or complementary charisms.

Then, maybe, another time we ourselves will come to the group with our own difficulty. As we explain it, we are aware of the concern of the others as they listen. One or two may be praying quietly for us while we are speaking, and we feel a liberation in knowing that we are not alone with our problems. If we have found it hard to seek God's will in the midst of our difficulty, we know that others are seeking his will for us.

During the prayers a thought expressed in a phrase or a quotation from the biblical passage we have been reading is incorporated in someone's spontaneous petition for us, and suddenly we see our dilemma in a fresh — and less threatening — perspective. We are made aware once more that the living Christ is with us in the midst of it, and that he has already conquered it through his cross and victory. We leave the meeting with an assurance that the problem is already solved by him.

I have said that certain personal problems are best discussed privately with a parish priest or minister or with one or two close friends. We have to be discerning in what we consider suitable for counselling and prayer in a group.

Similarly, groups have to be discerning in the effects their counselling and praying has on an individual member. We are all different in our psychological and spiritual makeup, and too much advice can be overwhelming for one individual. We should be alert to the subtle pressures that groups can exert on their members — pressures that are by no means always of the Holy Spirit.

When a piece of advice comes into my mind as I am listening to someone in counselling (with a group or privately), I usually hold it back to examine it. Is this your advice, Lord, or is it a human reaction in me to what I am hearing? Or is it both? Quite often at that moment another member of the group will ask a question or make a comment which indicates to me that similar advice has come into his mind, too.

Very occasionally, a completely new thought will come. After testing it before God, I wait for a suitable opportunity to speak it out in words which are given me as I do. This is how the charism of a word of knowledge operates, revealing facts we need to know to minister to others — facts we could not discover through the ordinary processes of discussion or investigation.

A group had been listening to two of its members describing a situation created by the unruliness of their teenage daughter. The couple were perplexed and blamed themselves, though they had no idea why the daughter should suddenly begin to act in this way. During the prayers that followed, one of the group had a word of knowledge about the girl's recent involvement in occult practices in the school. This word of knowledge gave the parents a clue to their problem. Eventually they were able to rescue her from these practices, pray with her for Christ's protection, and re-establish good relationships with her.

The subject of guidance, both for ourselves and for others, is notoriously difficult. Unfortunately there are a few charismatics who give the impression that they have a "hot line" to heaven and that they are able to proclaim the divine will for anyone at any time. And, equally unfortunately, there are others who are only too willing to be told what someone else thinks God wants them to do. Both kinds of people need to be treated warily by the rest of the group. The former have to be shown that the will of God is rarely revealed through instant oracles; the latter that Christian maturity depends on our being able to see God's purposes for ourselves and having the will to follow them in our own faith, not just because of what others say.

Where a group can help an individual is in praying about a matter and reaching a common mind with that member on what he or she should do. For a group of Christians to be able to say "it has seemed good to the Holy Spirit and to us" (Acts 15: 28) is a powerful indication that God is unfolding his will before them. But each member must be able to say this from his own heart and mind, not just because he does not wish to disagree with the rest.

When advice and guidance is sought in a group, then, a wise response will usually follow this pattern:

Let the individual talk about all aspects of his problem until both he and the group have a clear picture of what is involved.

Pray inwardly for discernment while he is doing this and openly for enlightenment when he has finished.

Wait until he has begun to move towards a solution himself (this may be at later meetings of the group) but do not in any way attempt to push him towards it.

Help him to test the solution by the means of grace given us by God (the teaching of the scriptures, prayers for guidance, going to Communion with the intention of seeking God's leading, the gifts of the Spirit).

See if both the individual and the group reach a harmonious sense of peace and satisfaction about the proposed solution.

Encourage the individual to accept the solution in the faith that the Holy Spirit will lead him out of the problem through it.

If this pattern is followed, it will guard the group against any tendency to try and force its own solution on the individual to whom it is ministering. The renewal movement has brought to many Christians a deeper sense of the victory of Christ into their lives. This is good. But it can have harmful effects if insensitive affirmations of triumphalism are made to those for whom that victory is not yet a reality. I have heard a number of horror stories about people with emotional, mental or physical problems being urged to "claim the victory of Christ" when they were quite incapable of doing that. The result has often been that their last state was worse than their first. We need to be patient — a fruit of the Spirit — with such individuals until they reach the point when they can receive Christ's guiding and healing power for themselves.

Perhaps a word is necessary about signs and "fleeces". Obviously God can use any means of revealing his will to us, and he does occasionally signify what he wants us to do by a remarkable ordering or changing of our circumstances. But such signs will nearly always confirm what he has been saying to us already, or what we have felt his will to be.

"Laying a fleece" means asking God to give a sign in a predetermined way, as when Gideon asked the Lord to indicate whether or not he would deliver Israel by leaving the ground dry underneath a fleece of wool left to get damp in the dew overnight (Judges 6: 36–40). Fleeces should only be used for big and important steps which we would not naturally take unless we have specific confirmation from God. Christians who have been called by God to do give up jobs and homes in order to engage in new ministries as ventures of faith have used "fleeces": to see such signs honoured is a remarkable encouragement when there is little else to show that the venture might be the Lord's will, after all!

CHAPTER 6

Testing the Spirits

TONGUES IS usually the first of the distinctly "pentecostal" gifts to be manifested in a charismatic prayer group. Members who have been praying quietly in tongues are led to speak them aloud. When this happens, the rest should expect an interpretation according to the apostle's instructions in 1 Corinthians 14: 27. When the tongues have finished, the leader may say a brief prayer, thanking God for this gift and asking him to speak so that the group may understand. He may also add a few words of explanation if there is anyone in the group, such as a guest, who is puzzled or perhaps alarmed by what they have heard.

Only as the group grows together will its members learn to judge when the Spirit is prompting them to use their "tongue". Experience teaches us when it seems right to speak out and when to keep silent. As a rough-and-ready guide, I would suggest that if you feel an inclination to speak aloud in tongues, first ask the Lord to take the inclination away from you if it is not of him. If it persists after that prayer, then speak out when an opportunity arises.

The interpretation may be given by the one who has spoken in tongues or by someone else. A few words or a complete sentence may be all that comes into our minds. Again we ask the Lord to take the words or the sentence away if they are not of him; and, again, if they persist, we speak them out in faith, trusting that the Lord will give us the remainder of the interpretation.

Interpretations are usually addressed to God — affirmations of faith and of praise, prayers of thanksgiving incorporating scriptural or liturgical material in an inspired way, canticles and songs. If the words of the interpretation are addressed to the group, then we can assume that it has taken the form of a simple prophecy — though we do not have to be too fussy about definitions.

A simple prophecy is given to us in much the same way as an interpretation. It is usually of an encouraging and upbuilding nature, not condemnatory (we can leave that kind of admonition to those who are thoroughly experienced in *charismata*). Before we deliver an interpretation or a prophecy, it is courtesy to the rest of the group to preface it with words such as "I believe the Lord is saying to us . . ."

I have often heard people say, "I wanted to pray aloud in tongues (or interpret or prophecy) but I didn't like to in case I was making it up." What was said in the previous chapter about trust and acceptance in a group is an answer. If we sincerely believe we can be used by the Lord in this way, we should be prepared to take a few risks and speak out. Only by trying will we learn the greater gift of discernment in what we are inspired by God to say.

Since we minister to one another in and through the body of Christ, each member of the group should be encouraged to see if he is being used by God for the manifestation of one or more of the spiritual gifts. If the same person always does the tongue-speaking or the prophesying in a group, the rest will tend to leave these charisms to him. We must not monopolise the exercise of particular gifts.

Besides, restraint can be rewarding. I was once at a prayer meeting when someone spoke in tongues. I believed I was given an interpretation, but as I had already spoken a simple prophecy earlier in the meeting, I kept silent and prayed that someone else would be given the charism.

Sure enough, after a long pause, a woman in the group began to interpret. I was delighted, for she had not done this before. She spoke several sentences authoritatively, calling us to seek God's peace beneath the disturbed waters of our lives. But then her voice faltered and she stopped. She had lost confidence in what she was doing.

At that moment, I was given the rest of the interpretation (as far as I can remember it was to the effect that to find peace with God we must be open to him so that he can purify and renew the lower levels of our personalities, for he brings light to things hidden in darkness and discloses the real purpose of our hearts). The incident not only helped several in the group; it also confirmed the woman in her belief that she could be God's instrument in this ministry.

If, after someone has spoken in tongues, an interpretation is not forthcoming, the leader can suggest that the group continues with its prayers in English. The interpretation may come later.

Someone in the group should make notes of interpretations and prophecies. Months — or years — later these notes can still be edifying, especially if we can look back and see that what we were told was fulfilled.

A few years before Reg and Lucia East left Mersea to found the Barnabas Fellowship at Whatcombe House, the prayer group that met in their vicarage was given numerous prophecies about the future community. Someone took a tape recorder to the meetings and switched it on when a prophecy was given. The prophecies were then typed out and the papers kept in a folder. That folder is now one of the Fellowship's most treasured possessions. We read it occasionally to see how some of the things that were recorded then have come to pass. It gives us an assurance that the establishment of the community is under God's hand and according to his will.

It is my experience that Paul's "two or at the most three" is about the maximum number of times that glossolalia with interpretations or the charism of prophecy can be manifested profitably in any one meeting. If they are used more often than that, it seems to me that they lose much of their inspiration.

Inspired Pictures

Charismatic groups experience inspired pictures or visions during their prayers. One member is given in his mind's eye a vivid scene or happening which he describes for the rest. Sometimes another member says that he can see it, too. The others ponder its meaning. Not infrequently the picture has an important significance for one or more in the group.

Pictures like these are not always spontaneous. I have sometimes tried to trace the origin of pictures I have been given back to a previous experience. Once I had a picture of darkened landscape overhung with heavy clouds until a bright light, coming from below the horizon, drove away the clouds until the sky was brilliant. My description of it served to encourage a man in the group who was encountering exceptional difficulties (I had a message from him later explaining this) but I was certain I had seen the landscape before. Suddenly, one day, I remembered. It had been the scene from the back window of the house I lived in as a boy. The dark clouds and the bright light I had seen one night during the war when the Luftwaffe was bombing Coventry twenty miles away.

People we know appear in the pictures. The Barnabas Fellowship spent three days in retreat at a Franciscan convent. We were impressed and humbled by the simple living standards of the sisters who made us so welcome there. A few weeks later, during our prayers, one of the community had a picture of a Franciscan sister kneeling before our Lord, holding up to him an empty begging bowl. Nearby was an affluent business man, taking no notice of Christ or the nun. The sister was asking Christ for financial aid. Christ pointed to the business man and that individual, taking out his cheque-book, wrote out a cheque and placed it in the begging bowl before he walked away.

At about that time we had been praying for money towards the cost of running conferences at Whatcombe, and we took the picture as a promise that help would be forthcoming, knowing that Christ could use even those who knew little of him for this purpose. Sure enough, before many weeks had passed, a number of generous cheques came through the post, some from people who were strangers to us.

Pictures are sometimes given like this when we pray with people. They can be a powerful assurance of divine aid when the one we minister to is seeking God's strengthening or healing.

A man asked me to lay hands on him while praying for God's grace as he took up a new job. It involved greater responsibility than he had held before, and for the first time he would have a number of men working under him. As a committed Christian he was anxious that he should be able to respond to the opportunities that God would give him to minister and witness in Christ's name.

While I was laying on hands, I saw in my mind's eye the interior of a beautiful cave. Among the stalactites and stalagmites two in particular attracted my attention. They were growing towards one another: the stalagmite on the floor of the cave was quite short, but a long, lovely stalactite was reaching down from the top of the cave towards it, the water dropping from its tip to the stalagmite and feeding it.

I described this picture to him, and later he told me God had spoken to him through it of the need to look upwards for divine grace continually and to be patient, moving only in the Lord's time.

"By the way," he added, "I used to be a keen potholer and I've been in caves like the one you described. How did you know?"

"I didn't," I replied.

During prayers in a conference I had a picture of a scarecrow in a field. It was made in the obvious way — two sticks fastened together to form the body and the arms, a turnip cut to look like a face, an ancient hat, and an old coat stuffed with straw with gloves attached to each end of the stick that made the arms. For a time I kept silent about the picture — it seemed slightly ludicrous to say anything about it — but eventually I decided to describe it to the conference. As I did so, it suddenly flashed into my mind that what I was looking at was the shape of a man on a cross — arms outstretched. And as I spoke I was led into a prayer asking God's forgiveness that, although we had died and risen sacramentally with Christ through baptism, too often our lives were only a grotesque distortion of the Son whom he had sent into the world to save us.

A long silence followed my description and my prayer, and then other penitential prayers followed. Afterwards two or three people in the conference told me they had found the picture leading them to examine their lives as baptised Christians with a fresh realisation of what the cross of Christ meant to them as sinners.

Gifts of Healing

Like guidance, healing is a notoriously difficult subject to talk about. I am only too conscious that if I write encouragingly about it I may give the impression that everyone on whom the members of the group lay their hands will be healed, and that if I write cautiously about it I may give the impression that anyone in a group who asks for the laying on of hands for healing must not hope for much to happen!

Yet neither of these is true. Quite apart from the way God uses the medical profession in healing the sick, he graciously and wonderfully answers prayer on behalf of sufferers.

In discussing intercession in a previous chapter, I pointed out the necessity for preparation, sensitivity and discernment before launching into petitions claiming the promises of Christ. This is especially necessary as we enter into a ministry of healing in a group. In an uprush of sympathy it is all too easy for someone to quote Mark 16: 18 ("They will lay their hands on the sick, and they will recover") and to blurt out, "I believe the Lord wants us to minister healing to him." The rest of the group chime in automatically, not wanting to miss the opportunity.

Usually it is wise to wait and ask questions. Is anyone else ministering to the sick person (the parish priest, for example)? What are the circumstances which led up to this illness? What is its nature? Is the Lord leading the sufferer through to some greater wholeness? Only when the group has prayed about questions like these is it right to ask God to heal. And it may well be that the one we pray for has to wait, too. A man was born blind "that the works of God might be made manifest in him" (John 9: 3), but he had to suffer darkness for many years first. When we embark on a ministry of healing, we enter into the mystery of Christ's own suffering for sinful humanity.

Having said this, however, I must add that spontaneous prayer for healing can be right, even if it is offered at a moment's notice without forethought. A group of the younger members of the Barnabas Fellowship were on a hill-walking holiday in Wales when one girl slipped and badly gashed her head. The wound bled and her friends bound it up as best they could with their emergency kit. One of them laid hands on her — she was lying on the ground partly dazed — and prayed that she would be healed. Then they helped her down the hill to the doctor's surgery in the nearest village. The leader of the party explained to the doctor what had happened as the bandage was removed — he broke off the story to tell the nurse to be careful for the cut was a nasty one — but when the girl's head was uncovered there was no trace of the wound. By the expression on the doctor's face it was apparent he was thinking this party was making a fuss about nothing!

When someone in a group asks for prayer and the laying on of hands, the leader can invite two members (different ones for each separate request, if possible) to minister on behalf of them all. The two stand on either side of the one who has requested ministry, laying their hands gently but firmly on his head and shoulders. They should take care not to put their hands on top of his head — hands placed in this position can feel heavy after quite a short time — but on the brow, at the side or at the back. I usually pray quietly in tongues at this point before beginning to intercede in English.

The prayer itself can be short but positive. Refer to one of the scriptural passages where Christ promises that the Father hears our requests and answers them, and then ask that the illness may be healed (or whatever is appropriate in the situation). Two people who are used to ministering together can share the prayer between them.

If the prayer is not obviously answered, the group should continue its ministry either until the illness is healed or until the one concerned feels that the group should suspend its ministry for a time.

Deliverance ministries are practised in a few groups. There is no doubt that many have been helped when Christians have prayed over them for their release from a spirit of evil which has distorted or gripped their lives. I have had only a limited knowledge of this kind of ministry, and I would advise any prayer group not to embark on it unless they have members who are experienced in it (with all the discernment and testing of guidance that I have just described).

A prayer for protection from the devil and all his

T–D

works can be offered for anyone when it is desired. Some groups ask for God's protection over their meeting when they assemble. One group experienced a series of unsatisfying meetings. No one could explain what the trouble was; they all knew that it was there when they came together. Eventually, the leader and his wife prayed before the meeting one evening that the devil would be banished from the room in which they met, and from that time the prayer group had no further trouble.

Discernment and Discipline

If spiritual gifts are to be listed in order of importance, I would put the charism of discernment towards the top. Without the illumination that comes from the Holy Spirit to distinguish between a gift which is of God and a gift which is false, the dangers of self-deception and evil influences increase enormously. When the Holy Spirit is active, we can be sure that the devil is also at work, seeking to sidetrack us away from God's path. Although we know that, in the end, the devices of Satan must fail, we can still be deceived by him; and the history of the renewal movement is littered with tragic cases which could have been avoided if Christians had prayed for and been open to the charism of discernment.

Whenever anyone is baptised in the Spirit, it is wise to tell them to seek for the gift of discernment above all others, drawing their attention to warnings in scripture about false revelations: "Do not quench the

Spirit, do not despise prophesying, but test everything; hold fast what is good, abstain from every form of evil" (1 Thessalonians 5: 19–22). The testing of the *charismata* helps us to accept what is of God's grace and to reject what is not. In 1 Corinthians 14 Paul applies as criteria of spiritual gifts intelligibility and the capability of building up the community; in I John 4 a theological test, the reality of the incarnation, is laid down, whereas in the *Didache* (an extra-canonical Christian handbook from the late New Testament period) it is in the correspondence of the prophet's own life to his teaching.

The group leader has a responsibility to see that charismatic manifestations are tested. While he will not want to criticise or denounce everything he sees or hears that he feels is not of God, he should retain a sensible neutrality about doubtful manifestations, intervening only if he believes they may lead to positive harm.

But how does discernment operate? All I can say in answer to a question like that is that there are occasions at prayer meetings or in counselling sessions when I have an inner conviction that something is not what it purports to be. It does not happen very often, but there is no mistaking this inner conviction when it comes. A prophecy may have been given which does not seem to call forth from me any response that I could believe was of the Spirit; a prayer may have been said that jars against what I believe to be God's will; a suggestion may have been made (perhaps prefaced by the words, "The Lord tells me . . .") which leaves me feeling uneasy.

If all this sounds too subjective — that it depends dangerously on my own feelings and not enough on the Spirit of God — then I can point to the ways in which the Church has discerned true *charismata* from counterfeit through the centuries:

(1) Nothing that comes from God will contradict the scriptures. When anyone says, "You'll never learn this from the Bible, it comes by revelation," then is the moment to be on our guard. All the truth we need is revealed in the scriptures. Every charism should be tested against passages such as the beatitudes of Christ, Paul's teaching on the primacy of love (I Corinthians 13) and the apostle's description of the fruit of the Spirit (Galatians 5: 22).

(2) Anything that is contrary to the teaching of the Church — taking into account the varying emphases of different Christian traditions — is likewise suspect. God sent his Spirit to guide his people into all truth, and any spirit that contradicts the sure guidance he has already given to the Church is not of him.

(3) *Charismata* which direct us to change the course of our lives (e.g., to give up our job) must be confirmed by other means before we act on them. It is not enough to accept one sentence in scripture or one remark in a prayer as a sure "sign" from God about what we are to do. We must wait until he confirms the guidance in other ways.

(4) The results of spiritual gifts are always purifying, loving, edifying, uniting and strengthening. Above all, they glorify God, Father, Son and Holy Spirit.

The advantage of seeking God's will in and

through a group of Christians is that there is some safety in numbers. It is more difficult for half-a-dozen to be deceived than one or two. Among the group there may well be mature Christians whose experience and wisdom in such matters is invaluable.

Finally, Christian ministry imposes the discipline of Christ on all those involved, both the one who accepts ministry and those who offer it.

(1) We should repent of all known sin and come in sincere penitence to Jesus Christ as our Saviour. If we are accustomed to making our confession, either formally before a priest or informally with Christian friends, we should do this beforehand.

(2) We should be absolutely positive in our faith in God. We should not come before him with doubts and questions, nor should we wait until our feelings are right. We should come praising and thanking him for his promises to fulfil our every need.

(3) We should continue to trust that God will heal us, or solve our problem, even when the answer to our prayers does not seem to be immediate.

(4) We should remember, above all, that our faith in God is basic; we are not required to have faith in the group or in any member of it. The lame man at the gate of the temple was seen "walking and praising God", *not* the apostles! (Acts 3: 9)

CHAPTER 7

Sharing in Ministry

So FAR in this book I have been largely concerned with the inner life of the charismatic prayer group; and I can imagine some readers asking themselves if I am encouraging the formation of little ghettos of Christians whose interests are centred on themselves.

This is certainly a danger. But, as I said earlier, a group that is concerned with its own affairs is hardly Christian and certainly not charismatic. It is called together by God for his purposes. Just as the individual Christian is equipped by the Spirit to minister to others in the name of Jesus, so the group of Christians are brought together so that they can minister to the wider congregation of God's people and, through the Church, to his world.

If I have concentrated on the subject of the formation and building up of the inner life of the prayer group, I have done this because that fellowship should bear fruit in the shape of a Spirit-directed ministry beyond its own membership. By learning to minister to one another, we are led into a ministry to others.

Shortly after the Barnabas Fellowship had begun its work in Whatcombe House, the Lord spoke to us during prayers one day: "I shall minister to others through you as you minister to one another."

At the time we were puzzled by this word of wisdom. It seemed as if God was urging us to pay more attention to ourselves than to our guests. But as the months went by, we came to realise what a wealth of truth the saying conveyed, for we saw that it was as we cared for each other in the community that the love of Jesus Christ was felt by those who stayed with us.

Had we looked more discerningly into the scriptures, we should have found this truth there! "By this all men will know that you are my disciples, if you have love for one another," said the Christ of the Fourth Gospel (John 13: 35). Paul echoed it in one of his prayers: "May the Lord make you increase and abound in love to one another and to all men" (I Thessalonians 3: 12) — the love of those closest to us in the Christian family ("one another") comes first and out of that flows the love of others ("all men").

It is in this ministry that the group discovers that what chapter thirteen of I Corinthians has to tell us about love is a more important manifestation of the Spirit than the gifts discussed in chapters twelve and fourteen!

Sharing with the Congregation

The ministry of the group beyond its own membership usually begins with the congregation of which its members are a part. If we visualise the group's ministry as ripples on a pond spreading out from the centre, then the first ripple of ministry from the group will probably touch the local church.

And the local church has a ministry to the group as well. Ministry, as we have seen, is a mutual sharing in the ministry of Jesus Christ, and through the link provided by the ordained clergy, the congregation is responsible for an apostolic oversight of the prayer group. It can offer its greater resources to the group when these are required in a shared ministry, and it can protect the group from those excesses which sometimes overcome any small company of enthusiasts if they become too detached from their parent body.

We have already noticed in an earlier chapter how important are the relationships between the parish priest or minister and the group leader in maintaining the unity of the group with the congregation. The concept of a shared ministry is a further step towards building up this unity. Through it members of the prayer group and members of the congregation come to recognise their mutual responsibility for one another along with their leaders. "We, though many, are one body in Christ, and individually members one of another" (Romans 12: 5). *Though many* — Paul was not speaking just of a small group or a single congregation!

The ministry of the individual group member to the congregation begins with the Sunday worship and other activities of the local church. The charismatic who sees the worship of the group as primary and that of the congregation as secondary, is taking a very limited and therefore distorted view of what the Church really is. Our relationships in the body of Christ are not confined to the few closest to us. We are members of a congregation in a neighbourhood, and the assembly of Christians in a neighbourhood — be it Anglican, Methodist, Roman Catholic, Baptist, United Reformed, etc. — is where we are identified as belonging to the Church. The focus of our Church membership is not the prayer group but the parish church or its equivalent.

Individuals will have to work out their priorities in these things. For example, an Anglican member of a prayer group may hesitate to stand for election to the parochial church council because that council's monthly meetings are on the same night of the week as the prayer group's gatherings. But before he decides he should bear in mind that God does not always call us to ministries which we find the most agreeable or spiritually uplifting. A parochial church council meeting may be far less inspiring to us personally than the weekly meeting of the prayer group, but our presence may be all the more urgently needed there.

Again, some charismatics tend to stand aloof from parochial activities which they regard as "unspiritual" — social functions, church cleaning, delivering the parish magazine, and so on. But spiritual gifts are not all of an exciting or dramatic kind. God is able to use these other, mundane ministries for his glory if we are prepared to trust him. A harvest supper can be transformed into an agape meal of thanksgiving if there are on the committee that planned it people who know how to lead spontaneous praying and singing (see pp. 124ff.) Church cleaning can be a valuable opportunity for befriending and counselling others in the congregation and ensuring that the building is worthy of the Gospel that is preached within it. And the door-to-door delivery of the parish magazine offers many opportunities of friendship and ministry.

Occasionally all the members of a prayer group have undertaken a ministry within the congregation as a body. I know of one group, formed when the vicar and a number in his congregation were baptised in the Spirit, which eventually became the parochial church council and which was responsible for most of the ministries carried on within the local church. But that is unusual. More often a group will undertake responsibility for a certain pastoral area, such as the oversight of the youth club or the organisation of the church's ministry to the sick.

But much of the ministry is done by individuals or couples with the support of the group.

Let me give two examples to illustrate what I mean.

A woman who was a member of a charismatic prayer group in a village was drawn by God to a concern for the transport drivers who pulled up at the roadside café some hundred yards from her cottage.

One day, very nervously, she went along to the café and began chatting to the only driver who happened to be there, introducing herself as a member of the church in the village. Quite rapidly she found opening up for her a ministry of counselling and witness among some of the most interesting people she had ever met in her life.

She was supported in this ministry through the prayer and practical help given to her by the members of the group. She would ring some of them up between meetings to ask for prayer before she visited the café (charismatic prayer groups have discovered the telephone as a means of corporate prayer outside meeting times and in moments of crisis: prayers over the phone can give a strong sense of unity) and her vicar warmly encouraged her.

Gradually the news of her ministry got about, and she was invited to address the diocesan committee for mission and unity on her experiences. At a time when the diocese was preparing itself for a year's mission, her experiment was voted as one of the most promising in the diocese and the broadsheet that she had had printed to give to drivers was distributed to every parish with the suggestion that others might do the same for the cafés in their area.

The second example is of a couple who attempted to do something similar among the young people who gathered in the pubs and coffee bars of a town centre on Sunday evenings. After prayer with a group, they went out with others to meet these young people and talk to them. Eventually they started a simple open-air service in a shopping precinct and found them-

selves joined week by week with a regular "congregation" of young people who had had very little
contact with formal Church life.

While it was summer these meetings were successful, but as winter approached the problem of
what to do next with the young people presented
itself. They found little support for their venture
from the various congregations represented in their
ecumenical prayer group.

The two examples illustrate the need for a ministry
shared between the individual, his group and his
congregation. The lady in the village embarked on her
ministry with the support of her group and her congregation (represented by the vicar) and, as that ministry developed, the whole diocese profited by her
initiative. The ministry of the couple was thwarted by
the lack of support, not from their prayer group, but
from their congregation.

Difficulties in Sharing Ministry

Most groups experience difficulties from time to
time in sharing in ministry with those beyond their
own membership. Two common difficulties are (1)
when they encounter suspicion or opposition from the
clergy and/or the local congregation, and (2) when
their members represent different denominations in
a neighbourhood.

The first difficulty can only be solved with much
patience and guidance from God. Suspicion or hos-
tility should provide the group with a powerful incentive to pray for the fruit of the Spirit. What they are

encountering basically is fear (though this fear may be disguised by a criticism that the group is being "cliquish" or that "tongues are not for today"). "There is no fear in love, but perfect love casts our fear" (I John 4: 18). Suggestions within the group that they should "leave the church" should be ignored unless there is clear and irrefutable guidance from God that this is his will.

This does not mean, of course, that the members of the group should not go elsewhere occasionally to seek ministry for themselves. If their own vicar and congregation will not help them, they cannot be blamed if they sometimes attend a larger prayer meeting in another parish or in a building belonging to another denomination. Most Christians "shop around" for ministry in special circumstances. But members should recognise that their own church has the first claim on their loyalties. It is tempting to attend "a more charismatic church" — but this is not the way God usually renews his people.

The second difficulty — that of an ecumenical prayer group — is extremely complex. Only a few points are made here. The leader of the group should seek to establish good relationships with the clergy of the different denominations, showing them that the group is not concerned with "sheep stealing". Equally, members should show their loyalty to their congregations by regarding the prayer groups as a means whereby they can fulfil their personal ministry in the local church.

The ministry of such a group may be rather different from that of the group in which all or most of the members attend the same church, but it will not be less rewarding. Tensions there will be — especially if individual members experience the reality of God's presence and grace in the group in a more powerful way than in their congregations — but these tensions are twinges of the great pain that Christian disunity causes throughout the body of Christ.

A prayer group which draws its membership from different denominations fosters the cause of Christian unity as long as its members identify themselves individually with their respective local churches. The Spirit will guide them in what they ought to do when problems arise — provided they are both discerning in his ways and obedient to their communities. Out of difficult situations such as these God has achieved ministries of reconciliation and demonstrations of power far greater than we could imagine.

The ecumenical movement in England has now passed the point at which negotiated schemes of reunion are regarded as the principal means through which Christ's disciples may be made one. It is widely recognised that real unity in the Spirit will only come when Christians of differing denominations in a neighbourhood do together all that can be done together without separating themselves from their churches. The next step beyond that is in God's hands.

If an ecumenical group is truly charismatic — in the sense that it manifests the love and unity of the Spirit among its members without creating further divisions in the Church — then it is a prophetic sign of the oneness in Christ into which God is gathering all his people.

Ministry in Mission

Beyond the local church is the great harvest-field of the world — the society in which we live and work and enjoy ourselves. Members of prayer groups should see themselves, as individuals and as a group, filled with the Spirit in order to be sent into the world to participate in what God is already doing there.

If we are open to him, God will show us how we are to share in his mission — in our homes, in our places of employment, in our neighbourhood, town, or country.

We should not overlook the obvious fact that if we have a job which brings us into contact with our fellow men and women, a gift of the Spirit may well be given to enable us to do that job properly and to minister to them as we do it. The same may be said of other encounters with people. Offices, shops, factories, businesses, farms, markets; social, educational, medical and industrial institutions; casual contacts with friends, the network of family relationships, involvement with parent-teacher associations, hospitals' leagues of friends, evening classes, clubs, voluntary bodies — in all places where people meet we shall find Jesus Christ working and inviting us to share in his ministry.

In that ministry we should be prepared for the pattern of the Lord's own experience to be ours, too.

There may be the initial joy and enthusiasm as we step out in the way along which he calls us. Things go well and we see the first fruits of the Spirit's work. This is the "Galilee" of our ministry.

Then there may be the difficulties, rejection, opposition, perhaps even costly personal sacrifices, when we feel we are alone and the temptation to withdraw is strong. This is our "journey to Jerusalem". Only the continued support of the prayer group keeps us going.

And then, after the tribulations, there will be the joy of seeing Christ's victory manifested in the changed lives of those to whom we have been ministering, or in the transformation of the circumstances in which we have been involved. This is our "road to Emmaus". We discover in a new way the risen Lord in our midst.

It is the same pattern which Paul recognised in his apostolic task, and he was inspired to write one of the most daring accounts of personal ministry that we can find:

> I rejoice in my sufferings for your sake, and in my flesh I complete what is lacking in Christ's afflictions for the sake of his body, that is, the church, of which I became a minister according to the divine office which was given to me for you, to make the word of God fully known, the mystery hidden for ages and generations but now made manifest to his saints (Colossians 1: 24–26).

Ministering for Personal Renewal

Among the people ministered to by the individual member of the prayer group there will be a few who will ask if he or she can receive the Holy Spirit more fully into their lives.

We probably experienced this ministry ourselves. It may be that we attended a meeting on the charismatic movement and at the end went forward for the laying on of hands, or it may be that a priest, a minister or a friend prayed with us privately. We shall, therefore, have had some practical experience to help us respond to this request. But if you are unsure what to do when someone asks you to pray with them for personal renewal, the following suggestions may be helpful.

If you have time, invite another member of the prayer group to minister with you.

Whether you minister with another or alone, see if you can elicit from the enquirer answers to a number of questions.

"Do you know what the baptism in the Spirit is?" Most enquirers would not ask for prayer for renewal if they had no knowledge of the subject, but misunderstandings abound. It is necessary to point out that baptism in the Spirit is a continuous process, that the work of Spirit began in their lives long before they were conscious of his presence, that he has been active in their baptism, confirmation, Communions, prayers, worship and life long before they felt any need of renewal. What we call baptism in the Spirit is a moment when we accept more fully what God promised through Christ when the Lord said, "You shall receive power when the Holy Spirit has come upon you" (Acts 1: 8). Roman Catholic charismatics in the U.S.A. have courses on

"Life in the Spirit" for instructing those who seek renewal to prepare them for the laying on of hands.

"Why do you wish to receive the baptism in the Spirit?" Often the reply is that it came from a desire to counter feelings of inadequacy or weakness as a Christian and to enter more fully into apostolic Christianity with its signs and wonders. The enquirer has to be gently led to the point where he can say that he wants more of the Spirit so that Jesus Christ may be glorified in his personal life. What we seek are not the spiritual gifts but the Giver!

"Do you truly repent of all your sins?" The conditions of ministry which I outlined at the end of the previous chapter apply with equal relevance when we are praying with someone for a renewal of the Spirit. They apply also to ourselves. We should ask God to take away all our offences in thought, word or deed, so that we can become worthy channels of his grace. We should also warn the enquirer that baptism in the Holy Spirit does not lead to a state of sinlessness. Rather, after renewal the Spirit will convict us of disobediences which we have not recognised in our lives before and he will sometimes bring to our remembrance old, half-forgotten sins which have damaged and which still damage our relations with God and with our fellow men.

"Do you commit yourself to Jesus Christ?" Christians have different ways of expressing their faith in their risen Lord. For some it will be in terms of "accepting Jesus Christ as Saviour"; for others it will be in terms of "holding to the faith of the Church". Since faith in Jesus Christ is a necessary condition for receiving the Spirit (Acts 2: 38; 8: 15–17, &c.), we have to assure ourselves that the enquirer is prepared to renew his baptismal confession before seeking a fresh anointing from the Spirit.

"Have you had any dealings with spiritualism, the occult, or similar practices?" When the Holy Spirit comes he searches the deep recesses of our personalities and previous involvement with such practices can cause reactions that can be dangerous — bitter self-accusation, irrational fear of the unknown, conviction of evil possession. If the enquirer admits that he has had dealings of this kind, we must be assured that he has renounced them and we must pray that he may be freed from any power that evil may have over him, claiming the protection of the blood of Jesus Christ. If in doubt, we should not proceed further until we have consulted someone experienced in the ministry of exorcism.

These questions are not intended to be put to the enquirer as a catechism but to mark out lines along which our preliminary conversation with him should follow. If we feel he needs time for further instruction or for seeking God's will, we can suggest that he comes to our prayer group for a few weeks.

When we are ready to pray together, we find a room or church where we are not likely to be disturbed. (When a man ministers to a woman it is wise to have another person, preferably another woman, with them.) We sit together and pray that God will reveal his love to us in a new way, meeting our needs with a fresh outpouring of his Spirit.

At this point I usually tell the one I am ministering

to that he may expect God to give him a new tongue with which to praise, but that this is not always the case. There is nothing in scripture that leads us to suppose that the gift of tongues always accompanies the anointing of the Spirit. I suggest that he should be prepared to open his mouth and move his lips when I lay hands on him, but not to force himself to make gibberish sounds.

After praying in tongues quietly for a while, I then stand beside him, lay hands firmly on his head in the manner I have already described, and ask God the Father to fill this disciple of Jesus Christ anew with his Spirit. I invoke one of those passages in which Christ promised that our requests will be answered if offered in his name ("If you then, who are evil, know how to give good gifts to your children, how much more will the heavenly Father give the Holy Spirit to those who ask him?" — Luke 11: 13.) Then, quietly and firmly, I pray that God will manifest himself in a new way.

Quite often the enquirer will begin to make strange noises. Sometimes the outpouring of the Spirit will be so powerful that he will lift his arms, stand up and shout praises to God, in English or in a tongue. Or the Spirit will enter him quietly, giving him a sure sense of peace and love. In other cases he will feel nothing — but the sense of peace and the gift of tongues comes days later (as it did in my own experience).

It is encouraging if he can express his thanks to God aloud, accepting the gift of the Spirit by faith, even if he has not felt moved in any way. We should end the proceedings with a prayer which we can say together, like the Lord's Prayer, and suggest that he rests in God, confident that Christ is present with him.

Those who are baptised in the Spirit as a result of our ministry should be steered towards a prayer group for reasons I have already described in this book.

CHAPTER 8

Breaking Bread Together

AFTER THEY have been meeting for a time, some charismatic prayer groups feel that they would like to celebrate the eucharist together. Members believe that the sacrament is a scriptural sign and seal of the unity that is growing among them in Christ. They do not usually want to do this at every meeting — only occasionally, perhaps every month or so.

It is not very satisfactory to use from beginning to end one of the liturgies authorised for services in church. To try and reproduce a church service in a domestic setting is artificial; something more informal and flexible is required. On the other hand, if the members attempt to devise their own eucharist, they will probably be disappointed with it — unless there happens to be in a group a priest or student with an appreciation and knowledge of the Church's liturgy. (Although the Holy Spirit can guide any group to celebrate the eucharist, his task is made easier if its members pay attention to the ways in which he has led the people of God to break bread together in the past!)

As a starting point, we might turn to the work of the Joint Liturgical Group, which was set up some years ago to study the common heritage of the Churches in their worship and to explore means of bringing the movement for liturgical revision in those Churches closer together. The J.L.G. represents Anglicans, Baptists, Methodists, Presbyterians, Roman Catholics and United Reformed churchmen. It has produced versions of the Calendar, the Lectionary and the Daily Office which have been used as the basis for new services, including those in the Church of England.

In 1972 the J.L.G. published a report entitled *Initiation and Eucharist* (S.P.C.K.) in which they analysed the essential liturgical material required to make up a baptismal and a eucharistic rite within the common traditions of Christendom. The basic elements which they prescribed for the eucharist form a valuable guide for any prayer group that is discussing how it can celebrate the Lord's Supper.

The J.L.G. point out that a eucharist is in two parts, a service of the word of God and a celebration of the Supper. The service of the word of God consists of the reading of scripture, the sermon and the intercessions; the celebration of the Supper consists of a taking of bread and wine, a prayer of thanksgiving, a breaking of bread and Communion.

Their report envisages a formal service in church. If we begin our prayer group meeting in the way I have described in the earlier chapters in this book, then we shall have fulfilled the basic elements of the service of the word of God in our reading of the Bible, our reflections upon it, and the intercessions that we offer in our prayers.

To this we add the second part, the celebration of the Supper. Besides the practical things which we shall need — the bread and wine and the various other things which I shall note in a moment — we shall also need to choose a prayer of thanksgiving. For this we can use any of the eucharistic prayers printed in the revised liturgies of the Churches in this country.

The Prayer of Thanksgiving

When the prayer of thanksgiving is said, it is usual for the one who presides over the celebration, the celebrant, to say the main section of it containing the narrative of the institution of the Supper. The rest of the group can join in the preface, the *Sanctus* ("Holy, Holy, Holy Lord . . ."), the acclamation ("Christ has died! Christ is risen! Christ will come again!") and the final doxology. But the prayer should be treated as a framework, not as a rigid formulary. For example, instead of saying the *Sanctus* together, the group might well sing a suitable chorus, such as the "Holy, Holy, Lord God Almighty" song from *Come Together*. Spontaneous thanksgivings can be added by individual members of the group at suitable points in the prayer. Once we become familiar with the wording and movement of the prayer, we shall soon be led by the Spirit to contribute to it ourselves in ways which enrich its themes and strengthen its intentions.

The eucharistic prayers of the Church of England's *Series Two* and *Series Three Orders for Holy Communion* are fairly satisfactory for this kind of celebration. So is the Eucharistic Prayer II in the Roman Catholic Church's *missa normativa*. When it is pastorally desirable for the service in the group to be associated closely in members' minds with the service in church, it is wise to use a formulary which is familiar to them. To gather round an ordinary table in a home and to hear the prayer of thanksgiving which they normally hear on Sunday mornings in church said over an ordinary plate and a cup gives them deeper insights into the nature of the Church's eucharistic celebrations.

But if our group is willing to experiment, then they might borrow from the new liturgies authorised for trial use in the Episcopal Church of the U.S.A., containing two prayers of thanksgiving which are very suitable for small group worship.

The first of these, Eucharistic Prayer B, allows the celebrant and those with him to extemporise their own introduction to the prayer (known technically as "the proper Preface"); then the celebrant continues:

We give you thanks, O Father,
for the goodness and love
which you have made known to us in creation,
in the calling of Israel,
in the words of the prophets,
and, above all, in Jesus your Son:

Who, on the night before he died for us,
took bread and gave thanks;
he broke it and gave it to his disciples, and said:
"This is my body which is for you:
do this for my memorial."
In the same way
he took the cup after supper and said:
"This cup is the new Covenant in my Blood.
Whenever you drink it,
do this for my memorial."

Remembering now his suffering and death,
and celebrating his resurrection,
and looking for his coming again
to fulfil all things according to your will,
we ask you, Father,
through the power of the Holy Spirit,
to accept and bless these Gifts.
Make us one with your Son in his sacrifice,
that his life may be renewed in us.

And therefore, Father, through Jesus your Son,
in whom we have been accepted and made your
    children,
by your life-giving Spirit
we offer our grateful thanks and say: Our Father. . . .

The second, Eucharistic Prayer D, is slightly longer
with an introductory dialogue.

Arrangements

The arrangements for the bread-breaking should be as simple as possible and yet orderly and reverent.

A table is prepared before the meeting with a clean cloth. On this is placed a suitable plate or paten for the bread and a cup or glass for the wine. When ordinary bread or a roll is used, it can be partially cut beforehand with a sharp knife so that it breaks easily into the required number of pieces for administering Communion to the members of the group. The cup is filled with wine. It is useful to have on the table a small jug of water and a paper napkin. The napkin, folded into a square, can be placed on top of the cup of wine to protect it from insects. One or two candles may be lit on the table if it is felt they are an aid to devotion.

After the scripture reading, the meditation and the intercessions, the celebrant stands behind the table facing the group. This is often a suitable moment to sing a hymn or a chorus. During the singing, the celebrant removes the napkin, adds a little water to the wine (the custom of a mixed chalice in the eucharist goes back to early times), and prepares to recite the prayer of thanksgiving.

When this is finished, he leads the group in the Lord's Prayer and administers Communion.

There are various ways of doing this:

(1) The celebrant receives Communion himself and then goes to each member of the group in turn, using words such as, "The Body of Christ keep you

in eternal life, Peter." After administering the Bread he also administers the Wine.

(2) The members of the group administer the sacrament to one another. The celebrant, after administering the Bread to the person on his right or left, hands the paten to them and they administer the Bread to the person next to them. The Wine is passed round in the same way. This method of giving and receiving the sacrament from one another has a special significance in a group which is learning to minister to one another through the guidance of the Holy Spirit.

(3) The Bread is administered as in (2) but the Wine is left on the table. After receiving the Bread, each communicant then approaches the table and takes the cup, administering the Wine to himself or herself. The advantage of this method is that it guards against the danger of spilling the Wine. (Should any of the Wine be spilled, the celebrant should immediately mop it up with the napkin.)

After the administration, the celebrant consumes what remains of the sacrament (or asks others to do so — if he has to drive after the meeting it is probably wise that he should not drink too much alcohol), brushing any crumbs that remain on the paten into the Wine with his finger. The cup or glass is then cleansed with a drop of water from the jug and lightly wiped with the napkin. The napkin should be burned later.

The J.L.G. do not include a general confession of sin among their essential elements for a eucharist, but in a note on the preparation of the people they point out that, before receiving Communion, we need to seek forgiveness, hear the assurance of pardon, and acknowledge anew our reconciliation with God and our unity with each other. I have already suggested that penitence has its place in charismatic prayer meetings. If an act of penitence has not been made spontaneously by the group before the service of the Supper, the leader can suggest that the group recites one of the formal confessions before the prayer of thanksgiving or before receiving Communion.

Nor does the J.L.G. include the Collect for the Day, the Creed, the Peace, or the Lord's Prayer among their essential elements. Most groups will probably want to use the Lord's Prayer at some point in the meeting. The Collect for the Day and the Creed can be incorporated into the service when occasion demands. A formal Peace is hardly necessary when people have already been together informally for an hour or more.

Agape Meals

When it is not possible to celebrate the eucharist other forms of meals may be used to invoke God's grace on his people as they meet together. These are usually known as "agape meals", the Greek word for "love" having been applied to the meal which seems to have accompanied the celebration of the eucharist in the apostolic Church (Acts 20: 7–12 and 1 Corinthians 11: 17–22, where this practice had been abused). Agape meals are derived from the Jewish custom of celebrating a festival by means of a sacred repast, like the Passover, with special blessings said over the various dishes — the form of meal, in fact, that Jesus shared with his disciples on the night that he was betrayed.

The varieties of agape meals are unlimited, and each group will evolve its own way of celebrating them. One form would be to prepare the meal beforehand in the dining-room and hold the first part of the meeting in the living-room. After the scripture-readings, the discussion, and the preliminary prayers, the group goes into the dining-room and the members sit at the table.

Instead of a short, normal grace, the leader pronounces over the food a longer prayer in the style of a Jewish prayer of blessing or a Christian eucharistic prayer.

"Blessed art thou, O Lord our God, King of the universe, who feedest the whole world with thy goodness, with grace, with loving-kindness and tender mercy; thou givest food to all flesh, for thy loving-kindness endureth for ever. Through thy goodness food has never failed us; may it not fail us for ever and ever for thy great name's sake, since thou feedest and sustainest all beings, and doest good unto all, and providest food for all thy creatures whom thou hast created."

The People:
"Blessed art thou, O Lord, who givest us food."

A eucharist prayer from the *Didache* (a

Christian manual from the end of the first or the beginning of the second century) can be adapted:

> We give thee thanks, our Father,
> for the life and knowledge
> thou hast revealed to us
> through Jesus, they Child.

The People:
> Glory to thee for ever.

> Just as this bread which we break
> once scattered over the hills,
> has been gathered and made one,
> so may thy Church too be assembled
> from the ends of the earth into thy kingdom.

The People:
> Glory to thee for ever. Amen.

The eucharistic prayer printed on p. 120–121 would also be suitable, provided the words of institution ("Who, on the night ... for my memorial") were omitted and it was understood that "Bless these gifts" referred to all the food on the table.

At the end of the meal a cup of wine can be passed round with words from the Jewish blessing:

> Blessed art thou, O Lord our God, eternal King,
> who createst the fruit of the vine.

Or the prayer over the cup from the *Didache*:

We give thee thanks, our Father,
for the holy vine of David thy servant,
that thou hast revealed to us
   through Jesus, thy child.

The People:
Glory to thee for ever.

The group is asked to continue during the meal the
discussion they have had over the scriptures, sharing
with one another in the things of God — not chatting
idly about anything. When the meal is over, there is a
further time of prayer and praise. The clearing of the
table and the washing up is done afterwards.

Agape meals provide a memorable way of mark-
ing special events in the group's life or in the
Church's year.

Singing

Both at ordinary meetings and at eucharists and
agape meals, singing is a popular way of praising
God and building up the group — provided it does
not annoy the neighbours!

Any attempt to "work up" devotion by the use of
choruses is deplorable, as I have already said, but
choruses introduced sensitively are particularly suitable as vehicles of corporate worship. Anyone can
start them and everyone can learn them. Usually they
are easy to memorise. Many groups collect their own
song-books, adding to their repertoire from hymn-
books, chorus-books, and from what they hear on
records and cassettes.

Singing in the spirit is one of the most beautiful ways of worshipping the Lord, especially at a eucharist, either as an extension of the *Sanctus* or the doxology in the prayer of thanksgiving, or at the end as an act of praise after Communion.

In this kind of praise each person sings to the Lord in a tongue, or in English, or hums, as the Spirit leads him, and the rest join in spontaneously with a free melody. The sounds blend together in a wonderful harmony. Sometimes it is soft and peaceful, at other times loud and powerful.

When the singing begins, we should hesitate for a moment, look at the Lord, and yield ourselves to him as we begin to sing. We keep our voices soft so that they do not dominate the voices of the group, letting the Spirit blend our voice with theirs. Occasionally it is followed by a period of silence and an interpretation — itself often a song inspired at that moment.

If I am presiding at a eucharist when singing in the spirit begins after the Communion, I sometimes read aloud over the softer passages texts from the scriptures we have been studying earlier in the evening. This recalls the word of the Lord to us in that service. (The post-Communion sentences of various traditional and modern liturgies perform a similar function.)

Problems of Order

In discussing the breaking of bread in the charismatic prayer group, I have avoided raising any of the problems of order which confront many Christians on

such occasions, especially when the group is ecumenical and when there is no ordained priest or minister present.

The problems arise from the fact that, since the
eucharist is a sacramental expression of the Church's
unity, most denominations surround its celebration
with certain safeguards (even if this is nothing more
than an invitation to "all who love the Lord" to receive Communion). In the Church of England and in
the Roman Catholic Church only an ordained bishop
or priest may preside at a eucharist. Roman Catholics may receive Communion only at Roman Catholic masses (and at the eucharist of certain Eastern
Churches in Communion with the see of Rome) and
non-Catholics may be admitted to Communion at
mass only in certain limited circumstances (though in
some parts of the world these circumstances are
much less limited now than they once were). Anglicans may receive Communion in any Christian
congregation where they are invited to do so, and
non-Anglicans may be admitted to Communion at
Anglican eucharists provided they are communicants
"in good standing" in their own congregations.

These disciplines create a sense of impatience in
some prayer groups and the suggestion is usually
made that the group should go ahead and break
bread together in the unity that the Spirit is giving its
members. To do this in defiance of Church order,
however, is to ignore the responsibility that we have
as a group to our clergy and congregations. The history of the Church is littered with the sad debris of
divisions that have been caused when order has

been broken, and a group which decides to "go it alone" will not be contributing to the glorification of Jesus Christ and the building up of his body.

The right thing to do, I am sure, is for the leader to talk the matter over with the clergy who are associated with the group. It is likely that various possibilities will present themselves.

(1) The priest himself, or a minister, will visit the group from time to time and preside over a celebration of the eucharist. In his office, he represents the wider Church and the concern which the congregation has for the group. Celebrations such as these can be very happy occasions, strengthening the unity between the group and the congregation.

(2) The leader, or someone in the group, may be ordained or authorised to preside at a celebration of the eucharist. The development of the auxiliary pastoral ministry in the Church of England and similar schemes in other Churches means that in future years this will become more feasible (see pp. 144–145).

(3) The leader presides over the celebration of a simple agape. When this is done, it should be made clear to the members and to the local clergy that it is not intended to be a form of the eucharist. In groups where there are Roman Catholics this form of celebration makes it possible for the Catholics to participate fully without being disobedient to the laws of their Church.

CHAPTER 9

Overseeing the Groups

THE SECOND CHAPTER of this book was addressed
specifically to those who found themselves acting as
leaders in a charismatic prayer group. This chapter is
addressed to clergy who find themselves having to
cope with charismatics and charismatic prayer
groups in their congregations. Others are welcome to
read it, of course! They may find it enlightening to
"listen in" to my side of the discussion with parish
priests and ministers!

If you have not yourself been involved in the charismatic movement in a close way, the first intimation
you are likely to receive that it is affecting members
of your congregation is a sudden, somewhat breath-
taking enthusiasm among one or two of them. They
will talk to you about a "pentecostal experience" in
which "Jesus became real". They will report at
length strange stories of what goes on in "charismatic
conferences" and "charismatic parishes". They will
urge you to read paperbacks (*As at the Beginning*,

Nine O'Clock in the Morning, perhaps *Greater Things than These!*) They will ask you to form a prayer group.

All this will certainly put you on your guard and cause you to treat these church members warily. They are not always the easiest people to deal with, especially if they think you are not "filled with the Spirit"! But it is well worth while bearing with their enthusiasm and accepting their estimate of you humbly. A considerable spiritual potential is being released through them and, if they are wisely guided, it can bring great blessings to the local church.

Those who have had an experience of renewal tend to think that everyone else in the congregation ought to have the same experience if the Holy Spirit is going to be real to them. It takes time for them to realise that the Spirit is not stereotyped in his dealings with us. After listening patiently to them, show them that you are pleased God has blessed them, gently remind them that the fruit of the Spirit is the authentic sign of his presence (Galatians 5: 22), and point out that the Church has always assumed that every one of her members is (or should be) filled with the Spirit and equipped to serve her Master. The texts of the baptism and confirmation services can be quoted to demonstrate this. You can also suggest that the New Testament teaches us to expect a wide diversity of charisms among the people of God and that simple acts of hospitality and administration are also regarded as spiritual gifts.

If possible, accede to their request for a prayer

group and form one, using them as the basis of membership. Lead it yourself but allow freedom in matters such as a choice of Bible readings and expressions of prayer. Show that you are present as a learner as well as a leader. Talk about it to other clergy who are involved with charismatic prayer groups. You may find after a few months that the leadership can be handed over to one of the lay members of the group.

The Minister and the Leader

In Anglican and Roman Catholic churches, where congregations look to their parish priest as their leader, lay leadership is still slightly suspect, in spite of the use of readers, catechists, and lay chairmen of synods and committees. In the Free Churches leadership is more diffused among the laity, though not always with the happiest results.

The leader of a charismatic prayer group will, therefore, need your support and pastoral care. In this way you manifest the congregation's ministry of "oversight" to the group and its leader.

In the list of guidelines on the discernment of leaders, I suggested that one of these was the candidate's acceptability to the congregation represented by the parish priest or minister (p. 33). If groups follow this guideline, it should present you with an admirable opportunity for establishing good relationships with the leaders. When a number of such leaders emerge among the groups in your congregation, you will find yourself the head of a "team ministry" from which you yourself may derive much personal support and encouragement.

Clergy and prayer group leaders should meet regularly to pray together, to discuss the ministry of the groups, and to relate their activities to the wider mission of the local church. The priest can advise the leaders on how to tackle pastoral or administrative problems which arise through tehe groups; the leaders can keep the priest in touch with what is happening among the members of the groups, drawing him into matters which he is better equipped to deal with through his theological training and pastoral experience.

While you are leader of a group yourself, most of the problems which can arise between a group and a congregation are avoided. The congregation see the group as part of your total ministry to them and — except for petty jealousies — are content that it should be so. When a group has its own lay leader, however, tensions can arise between the group and the congregation and one of the first to sense these tensions will be you!

This is where your relationship with the leader is so important. I have already given one example of how this relationship is tested in coping with an imaginary tension between a group and a congregation (pp. 36–37). As long as the parish priest or minister and the leader trust one another, no problem between the congregation and the prayer group is insoluble.

In spite of all your pastoral care, however, it sometimes happens that a charismatic group decides to "go it alone" and begins to break away from the congregation. If this should happen to a group in your church, try not to resent their schismatic tendencies and keep in touch, either by visiting them during their meetings or by entrusting this task to a conscientious and reliable layman. If you, as a parish priest or minister, show the group that you still regard them as your pastoral responsibility, they are almost certain in time to begin to respond to your love and concern for them.

It may be that for a considerable period you will have to treat them as a separate group — as you would if you were, for example, the part-time chaplain of a hospital, where the staff have very little connection with the congregation in your church. It may be that in time the group and its leader will run into difficulties. You will then be in a strategic position to step in as adviser and mediator. Few groups can go it alone for long. They eventually need ministry from others outside their membership. This is one of the ways in which the Lord reminds them that his family is bigger than their own circle. By virtue of your office, you can be the representative of that bigger family when the erring group realises what God is saying to them.

Training for Leaders

Much can be done to assist group life and ministry by arranging training courses for the leaders as soon as they feel the need for these. While selected reading helps, nothing can replace the teaching experience of weekend conferences or holiday courses for lay leaders in the congregation.

Sensitivity training is especially valuable. While God certainly equips in wonderful ways those whom he calls to lead, this does not mean that we should neglect what means of training are available to us through the adult education departments of the Churches. Most of them organise courses which provide insights into one's own and to other people's behaviour in small group situations.

Courses in group sensitivity usually require several days' residence at a training centre. Not everyone who leads a group will be able to go on one of these. A few may be fortunate enough to be sent on such courses by their employers as part of their in-service training in their career.

Care has to be taken in selecting individuals to go on these courses. Not everyone is psychologically fitted for the experience (though anyone who becomes a group leader as a result of the guidelines I have suggested is not likely to come within this category). Those who organise the courses will advise on this.

When it is not possible for group leaders to go on courses of this kind, a simple introduction to the need for sensitivity can be offered on a do-it-yourself pattern. The following six sessions have been used by me for a number of lay men and women who were in leadership positions in the parish (not only prayer group leaders but also the chairman of an organisation and an official in a scout and guide parents' association). Trainees should be asked to give the sessions a high priority in their engagements and attend each one. It assists the trainees if they can meet on "neutral territory" — a sitting-room in a club or an empty common room in a college building.

Ensure each session ends with a period of corporate prayer and encourage the trainees to use that time to offer to God what they have learned in the session to further their task as leaders in the Church.

I have only outlined the content of each session: it can be modified according to circumstances. Although you are in the position of instructor or consultant, endeavour to identify yourself as closely with the trainees as possible, showing that you are willing to expose yourself to the demands of the course along with them and that you are in no way being judgmental of their reactions to it.

Session 1. You welcome the trainees to the course and explain that its object is to help them to be more sensitive to peoples' feelings in small-group and inter-group situations. You have brought them into a small-group situation and they themselves are going to learn by analysing their own reactions in the group which they have formed. You warn them that there may be times when they feel a little uncomfortable or exposed, but you go on to point out that it is only when we ourselves begin to feel the things that others feel that we can really learn how to help them.

After this introduction, you invite them to discuss the difficulties they experience in the groups of which they are members and you assist them to analyse their thoughts and feelings. Why do you imagine that So-and-so doesn't like you? What is it about long silences that make you feel uneasy?

Half-way through the first session you invite them to take part in an exercise which, you explain, should help them to be more aware of themselves and of others in a group situation. You ask them to talk among themselves but to ignore you completely.

At first they may be shy of this — or act awkwardly, with sidelong glances at you and cryptic remarks. Take no notice of these reactions but observe how each trainee behaves. After a few minutes they will probably begin to forget your presence and discuss some topic that one of them brings up. Give them about twenty minutes and then stop their conversation abruptly. Ask each trainee to describe frankly how he felt. It is likely that one or two actually said little, and one of these may confess to rising feelings of anger that the rest of the group ignored him. You can point out to the trainees that not to notice one or two were uninvolved in the conversation was an oversight on their part: as leaders they should be alert to do what they can to involve everyone.

Session 2. The previous week's exercise is repeated but you explain that while you keep silent you are going to make some notes. You encourage the trainees to start talking again (you could give them a controversial subject to discuss) and when they have become engaged in the discussion, begin your notes.

On your pad you draw a diagram representing the group — a small square for every person's chair and their name beside it. As they speak you draw lines representing the "direction" of their words. For example, if John addresses a remark to Mary, you draw a line with an arrow from John's square to Mary's on your diagram; if John's remark is addressed to the group in general, then you draw the line from John's square to the centre of the diagram. (You can devise your own method for representing other things, such as jokes or asides.)

After about twenty minutes, you stop the conversation and show the diagram to the group. It is often very evident from the line-drawings how certain people have monopolised the conversation, "paired" with someone else in the group, kept aloof from the discussion, and so on.

Next, you join the group yourself and invite someone else to act as observer. This not only gives a trainee the opportunity to learn by observation, but it also shows that you are willing to submit to the same exercise yourself.

In any of these exercises there may be long, awkward pauses, perhaps a few giggles and uneasy backchat. Do not be worried about these. When the exercise is over, it will be useful to examine the reasons for awkward pauses in groups.

After this session individual trainees may want to bring up problems they are experiencing in their own groups, and time should be allowed for this.

Session 3. Take a tape or a cassette-recorder to the

meeting and tell the trainees that you are going to record half-an-hour's discussion. You switch it on and introduce a controversial topic. They may feel anxious about the microphone, but you will probably be able to distract their attention from it by making provoking statements. If the argument develops, do not try to stop it immediately. See if anyone else attempts to reconcile differing viewpoints.

The tape is then played back to the group and they listen to what was recorded. Some will be startled when they hear how belligerent they sounded. You can award "marks" to those who contributed positively to the discussion — introduced new factors in the conversation, brought points together, recapitulated an argument, acted as mediator, and so on. The value of a tape is that sections can be run back and replayed so that the part taken by different people in the discussion can be analysed more closely.

Session 4. At the beginning of the session you announce that one of the trainees is to take the chair and lead the group in prayer. You hand him a piece of paper on which you have listed the names of all those in the group. You tell him that he is to ask each person what he would like to pray about, to start the prayers, and to encourage each to participate, including yourself!

This can be an awkward session — perhaps the most difficult yet — and the idea that prayer can be used as material in an experimental way like this is revolting at first to some. But the art of leading prayer is important for the trainees and it is worth while taking risks in order to help them to feel more competent at it.

At the end discuss the prayers and their reactions to them, trying to discover why some find it so difficult to participate in extemporary prayer. Some of the points made in Chapter 4 can be raised.

Session 5. You divide the trainees into two subgroups, one consisting of only two or three people (with four or five trainees it is not so easy to do this exercise: ideally there should be a large sub-group of four or more and a small sub-group of two or three). You tell them that they are to make notes on a piece of paper about the reactions of the people in the other sub-group to the course, and then you sit the sub-groups at the opposite ends of the room or send one into another room.

The purpose of this exercise is to give the trainees some experience of the tensions that can arise between groups. They all know that the people in the other group are talking about them personally and this can create a feeling of unease in some, contributing to a rise in tension.

After a while, you call the sub-groups together and ask each person in them, not what he wrote in his notes, but how he felt during the session. Usually feelings vary. One or two say they adopted a couldn't-care-less attitude; others say they felt resentful. Somebody may admit that he was not able to think very clearly because he was wondering what the other sub-group was saying about him!

You use the material they present to discuss the

problem of inter-group relationships and to point out how misunderstandings and suspicions can arise (usually quite unjustifiably) because the members of one group are not accurately informed about what is being said in another. Feelings of isolation and rejection overshadow a small group in its relationships with a larger group when the lines of communication are not kept open.

The session can end with a discussion on the relationships between the groups which the trainees lead and the congregation of which they are a part, with suggestions for improving these links.

Session 6. You announce that, as this is the final session, you want to record a discussion of the trainees' reactions to the course as a whole.

This time you exercise all your skill as a chairman to draw individuals out, help them to express themselves, draw conclusions together, and set out opposing viewpoints. After half-an-hour or so of this, you play the recording back and invite the group to comment on your efforts as a chairman. Did what you said facilitate the discussion or did it block it? Did individuals feel that they had an opportunity to contribute, or did they feel you checked them before they had been able to express all that they wished to say?

It does not matter whether or not you happen to be a good chairman. Your efforts provide the audio-aid for the session — and you may find that you learn much about yourself!

Leading Elsewhere

Once an individual or a couple have been used by God in the ministry of leadership in one group, they are often led to a similar ministry elsewhere. It does not always follow that those who lead a group in one congregation are necessarily acceptable as leaders in another group, of course, but generally speaking experienced group leaders frequently find themselves in a similar position if they move their home and attach themselves to another congregation. I have met a number of individuals and couples who, having started a prayer group in their home, moved house and initiated another group. In fact a generation of Christians is arising for whom prayer in a group is as normal a feature of their life-style as worship in church on Sundays. If they do not find a prayer group in their new local church, they start one! One couple, having been leaders both in England and abroad, formed a daily prayer group in their cabin on board ship during the long voyage back to England!

If a former prayer group leader moves into your neighbourhood and joins your church, it is advisable to wait for a while to see how the congregation react to him (or them) before suggesting he initiates and leads a new prayer group. He may be quite happy (and perhaps relieved!) to join an existing group as a member. If the Lord intends to use him in a new group, then the guidelines will appear as I have suggested earlier.

Group Leaders and Ordination

As the life of the charismatic prayer group matures and its ministry is blessed by God, the question may arise, Will that group be more effective under the Spirit if its leader is ordained?

Some of the ways in which a group may develop prompts this question. In a previous chapter I have already discussed the desire to celebrate the eucharist in groups. In the next chapter I shall outline other developments, such as house churches and the establishment of a permanent community, which may call for the ministry of an ordained man in the group.

It is not for me to answer the question. I am only concerned that it should be raised.

It is interesting to note, however, that all the Churches in England and elsewhere are exploring ways of extending the ordained Ministry into what is variously called "the part-time priesthood", "the auxiliary pastoral ministry", and "the sector ministry". The guidelines which I have suggested in the choice of a leader for a prayer group are also the traditional guidelines behind the Church's selection of candidates for its ordained Ministry. This seems to indicate that the connection between the emergence of a man with the spiritual gift of leadership in a group and the question of his ordination may be closer than the Church of England allows for in her selection policy.

We are on the verge of a large topic which we cannot pursue here. But it is perhaps worth while raising the question of the training for ordination of the kind of men that often emerge as leaders of groups. Some of them adapt themselves happily to the existing ordination courses devised for candidates for the auxiliary ministry. They dip into the various subjects studied at greater depth in our theological colleges and pass an examination or qualify by means of essays. But others do not fit into this kind of course. Their training needs to be more practical — leading them to a deeper understanding of the ministry they are already exercising in the group. To remove them from the group for a lengthy course involving much evening or weekend study is hardly the best way to equip them to serve the group which looks to them as a mini-pastor.

If you, as a Church of England vicar, think of a prayer group leader as a possible ordination candidate, it might be advisable to negotiate with the bishop and the director of training for the auxiliary pastoral ministry in the diocese to see if a course cannot be devised which interferes as little as possible with the leader's continuing ministry in his group. The situation in the Church of England is still fluid enough for experimentation, and some dioceses are showing that they are well aware of these opportunities.

CHAPTER 10

Following the Spirit

THE PRAYER GROUP is established, the leader is gaining experience, and the ministry of the group is emerging out of its response to the word of God and its fellowship of prayer. What are we to expect next? What will be the future of the group?

Its future — like its formation and establishment — is in the hands of God. If God called the group together, he has a purpose for it, and its members should pray to be in that purpose, following the Spirit.

I shall end this book by outlining a few of the paths along which the Spirit has led groups I have known. In doing so, I am not suggesting that your group must necessarily expect to be led along one or other of these paths. God may have something quite different in store for you. But the outlines may help you to be more discerning as you seek the Spirit's guidance, and they may enable you to see ways that are open to the charismatic prayer group within the wider ministry and mission of Christ's Church in the world.

Groups that Scatter

One possibility is that, after meeting for a few months, the members of the group scatter and it ceases to exist. I have put this possibility first because in the eyes of some it would appear to be a sign of failure. But such an assumption is very man-centred. God can achieve much in the lives of individuals through the brief encounter of Christians in groups — the results of conferences are a remarkable witness to that. A short experience of this kind of fellowship can be just what certain individuals require as the Spirit leads them into a new ministry.

We live in a highly mobile society, and among any group of eight or ten people, one, two or three of them are likely to leave a neighbourhood and go and live elsewhere in the course of a year. And there is a vast, fluid population of students and other young people — from whom many charismatic prayer groups draw their membership — always on the move. If the number of people forming a prayer group dwindles and replacements are not forthcoming, those who survive ought to consider if the time has come for them to cease meeting, at least for a season.

Generally speaking, most Church activities outlast their usefulness. There is a pathetic reluctance to close meetings down long after they have ceased to serve a pastoral purpose. The gift of discernment is necessary to discover whether God is saying that his purposes for a prayer group are over and he is calling its members to scatter.

The scattering of a group, like the scattering of the early Church from Jerusalem, can be widely beneficial. I have known keen members of prayer groups move to other localities, even to other countries overseas, and initiate meetings in their new homes, taking with them all that they have learned in their original groups.

Individuals who have matured in Christ as a result of attendance at a prayer group have been used by God in other spheres of ministry — notably in full-time work for the Church in an official capacity or on a living-by-faith basis. Indeed, one of the most valuable fruits of a prayer group is its tendency to send out members to work for the Lord. Other individuals continue as more committed members of their local congregations, their experience of God's grace deepened as a result of a few months' meeting with others in a group for discussion, prayer, and ministry to one another.

We must not assume that the closing of a group after its initiation is necessarily a regrettable event. Its brief existence may have been as much in the purposes of God as its genesis.

Groups that Multiply

Another possibility is that a group subdivides into two, sharing in some activities together at first, but gradually separating until a new group has emerged which continues with its own meetings. The reason for subdividing is usually that the membership of the original group gets too large — once the number rises above ten or a dozen the character of the group changes and it loses its face-to-face intimacy.

But it may also happen when some members in the original group feel that they must separate to pursue a different life-style or ministry. This may manifest itself first in a difference of opinion among the members about an important matter of policy. Differences of opinion should not in themselves be the cause of a group's dividing. It is better to pray about the differences and live with them until it becomes clear to all the members that a group's dividing is a response to God's call, not a reaction among those who disagree.

When a group subdivides, everything hinges on the emergence of a leader for the new group — and in this case what was said about leadership earlier in this book is vitally relevant. While the original group has been meeting with a gifted leader, the need for another leader will not be apparent. But once the division has been made, the new group will be lost and will disintegrate if it does not find a leader among its members.

Each group has a character of its own. Once a number of members have separated from the original group, their life-style will probably be quite distinct from those of the group that they have left. It is in this way that the Church follows the Holy Spirit into new opportunities for sharing in Christ's ministry and mission.

The members of different groups may still come together occasionally, of course, not only in the congregation on Sundays but also on other occasions, such as prayer meetings (see below pp. 151-153), and it is possible for an individual to belong to more than one group. But the effectiveness of a group's ministry, like that of an individual, tends to diminish if members' commitments are diversified among different meetings. Most individuals can offer more of themselves to the Lord and to other Christians if they regard one congregation and one group within that congregation as their basic commitment.

People who have been meeting together for some time resist suggestions that they should break up into smaller gatherings, and it is foolish for any leader or handful of members to try and force such a change on a group that does not want it. If the numbers increase so that it is obvious the group must be divided, all the members will in time see the need for the change and agree to it, however regretfully. The process of separation can then be done carefully, respecting each individual's wishes.

The Prayer Meeting

Yet another possibility is that the prayer group grows in numbers until it is compelled to shift its meeting-place from a house into a church building or a hall. This happened to the first charismatic prayer group which met in Kimmage Manor, the house of the Holy Ghost Fathers in Dublin. Within months its membership swelled into hundreds and it had to move from one hall to another, seeking larger accommodation. It is in this way that a prayer group becomes a prayer meeting.

The prayer meeting is like a large-scale prayer group, but with important differences. Because of its size, the intimate fellowship of the group is lost. Sharing is limited. There may be testimonies from individuals and prayers, including tongues, interpretations and prophecies, but only by a few. Most who attend participate only passively.

The main purpose of the meeting is worship, with a focus on praise. Singing builds up the spirit of fellowship in the gathering, led by a pianist or a guitar group, and then the meeting moves into corporate prayer.

The "dictatorial" style of leadership, discussed earlier, is required. The one who presides must be in firm control. He must be prepared to deal firmly with any exhibitionist tendencies among those present, making sure that the free periods in the meeting are not monopolised by a few. He must know when to move from one stage to the next — from chorus-singing to prayer, from scripture reading to address, from prayers of intercession to prayers of praise, and so on — and he must be sensitive to the movement of the Spirit within the meeting, so that he is able to modify his plans to include unexpected elements.

His attitude is one of relaxed friendliness and expectancy. His opening remarks will do much to put strangers at ease. A speaker may have been invited to address the meeting, and it is the task of the one who presides to introduce him. But he will also be on the look-out for the individual in the audience whom he knows he can call forward to give a short testimony. (One of the hazards I run if I go to a prayer meeting personally is that, if I am recognised by those on the platform, I am usually invited to step forward and to say something about the Barnabas Fellowship at Whatcombe House!)

Ministry to individual needs is more limited in the prayer meeting, though people can be encouraged to pray for one another by providing an opportunity for the whole meeting to divide informally into little groups for ten minutes or so during the course of the evening. The leader invites everyone to stand and shake hands with those nearest to them, in front and behind as well as on either side. He then tells them to stand in circles of four or five and to ask for prayer one by one in their little groups for whatever need they have. Many have been helped by this simple device. The leader judges when it is right to summon people to sit again and to resume the meeting.

Prayer meetings have three valuable functions:

(1) They enable charismatic prayer groups to meet together in a more informal way than is usually possible in a church service. Prayer meetings should be supported by prayer and preparation from prayer groups, and it may well be that, when a group grows in size so that it becomes a meeting, some of the original group should continue to assemble separately to pray for the meeting.

(2) They bring a new spirit of expectancy and freedom to the normal Sunday worship of the local church. It might be argued that they detract from the centrality of the Sunday worship and perhaps compete with it, but this is not in fact the case. The experience of worship in a prayer meeting enables

participants to enter more fully into the formal structures of the Church's liturgy with considerable
benefit for everyone concerned.

(3) They provide an opportunity for enquirers to
learn more about the gifts of the Spirit and other
distinctive features of the charismatic movement.

The House Church

And yet another possibility is that the charismatic
prayer group becomes a house church.

The term "house church" denotes a group of
Christians whose life and worship is centred elsewhere
than in a normal church building. It is, in fact, a
"congregation" of the local church. It may meet in an
ordinary house; equally it may meet elsewhere, such
as a room in an institution like a college or a hospital.
It could also be the form of a local church in a new
housing area before a special building is erected.

The geographical locality, the social circumstances, or the life-style of this group of Christians
makes it unrealistic for them to identify themselves
with an existing congregation. They have their own
priest or minister (who may also be partially committed to other house churches or to other congregations).

When this happens, much of what I have said in a
previous chapter about the group member's responsibility to the local congregation no longer
applies. He is still part of the wider Church, of
course, but since his local church is now the same as
his prayer group, his responsibility towards other

local churches is on a congregation-to-congregation basis, not a group-to-congregation one.

If a prayer group does become a house church, then there is a strong case for the ordination of the leader or of some other suitable person that it may be a gathering in which, according to the Articles of Religion, "the pure Word of God is preached, and the Sacraments be duly ministered according to Christ's ordinance in all those things that of necessity are requisite to the same".

The Community

Our last possibility — in many ways the most interesting — is that the charismatic prayer group becomes a quasi-permanent community, its members drawn together by the Holy Spirit in such a way that they feel the desire to share in some form of communal life, either under one roof or in near proximity to each other.

The simplest way of doing this is by renting or acquiring a large property where two or three families or a family and several single adults can live together, some members going out to work, the remainder looking after the home and engaging in various forms of full-time ministry. The Church of the Holy Redeemer, Houston, Texas, is one of the most well-known examples of this development, although many others may be found now, both in England and in other parts of the world.

In our cities the big town house, built in the last century to accommodate a family with a domestic staff, is ideal for this purpose. In the newer suburbs communities are being housed in semi-detached dwellings either by adding extensions or by purchasing two nextdoor to one another and making them into one.

The leader of the group becomes the head of the community, and the community pursues its ministry either as part of the local church or as a local congregation in itself. It can be a powerful ministering and missionary unit in modern society.

Conclusion

THESE, THEN, are some of the ways in which charismatic prayer groups are formed and develop as
they follow the leading of the Spirit. But, as I said in
the introduction to this book, these descriptions are
only suggestions. They do not provide a blue print for
any single prayer group. It is for the reader to discern
what he can use and what he can disregard as he
applies what I have written to his own circumstances.

We must not imagine that every group will be led
along one of the paths that I have outlined in the last
chapter. For many of our groups God's purposes
will be fulfilled if we meet faithfully each week or
fortnight, receiving God's word together, praying
together, and sharing in Christ's ministry among ourselves and within our local church.

Nor must we imagine that every member of
the congregation ought to belong to a prayer
group.

There are some who are called by God to be "loners" in his service, at least for a period in their lives. The ancient eremitic vocation is continued by those who make a solitary witness to Jesus Christ in the deserts of modern society with only the slightest connections with their fellow believers.

There are some who receive support from Christian families and Christian friends in the congregation and who do not feel the need for the fellowship offered by a prayer group.

And, to be frank, there are some for whom the thought of being involved in closer relationship with other Christians is personally threatening. Among our congregations there are still those who fear the demands that might be made on them by a group of fellow believers — or, perhaps more accurately, who fear the demands that might be made on them by Jesus Christ through a group of his disciples — and prefer to regard their membership of the Church as a casual association rather than a commitment to a community.

But there are still many more who seek the fellowship of the charismatic prayer group which offers a deeper form of fellowship (*koinonia*) and a more gifted form of ministry (*diakonia*) than is found in some congregations these days.

Perhaps we can regard these groups as earlier generations of Christians learned to regard the religious orders in their midst.

It is a scriptural principle that God calls some of his servants to special tasks for the good of the whole Church. The prophets were among the first to realise that they were being called to a mode of living that was, in itself, a sign to call God's people.

Through the centuries down to our own day the religious orders have been recognised as a prophetic sign, pointing the rest of the Christian community to the ultimate demands of the Gospel in a life based on vows of obedience, poverty and chastity. Their witness has encouraged countless numbers of other Christians in their calling.

The charismatic prayer group, obediently following the Spirit in its devotion and ministry, is a similar kind of prophetic sign to the whole body of Christ. By its existence it recalls the Church to truths about the nature of Christian fellowship; by its service it encourages every Christian to realise the charismatic nature of Church membership.

It is a sign that God gathers his people together that Jesus Christ may baptise them with the Holy Spirit, that his name may be glorified and his Church built up.